GOD HAS SMILED ON ME

GOD HAS SMILED ON ME

A Tribute to a Black Father who Stayed
and a Tribute to all Black Fathers who Stay

DANIEL WHYTE III

GOD HAS SMILED ON ME

Cover Design by Atinad Designs.

Copyright 2009
TORCH LEGACY PUBLICATIONS: ATLANTA, GEORGIA;
DALLAS, TEXAS; BROOKLYN, NEW YORK

First Printing 2009

The Bible quotations in this volume are from the King James Version of the Bible.

The name TORCH LEGACY PUBLICATIONS and its logo are registered as a trademark in the U.S. patent office.

ISBN-13: 978-0-615-30191-4

Printed in the U.S.A.

Cover Photos:
Picture #1: Daniel White, Jr., Daniel White III, and Daniel White IV at Daniel White III's graduation from Bethany Divinity College and Seminary.
Picture #2: Daniel White, Jr., in a recording studio.

DEDICATION

This book is lovingly dedicated to my
grandmother, "Mother Tempie" White,
whom my father loved very much.
And to my favorite aunt, Rebekah Credle,
who single-handedly successfully raised five
boys who all graduated from college.

CONTENTS

ACKNOWLEDGEMENTS

First of all, I wish to thank God for allowing me the joy and privilege to do such a work as this. I also thank the Lord for a father who stayed and did the best he could.

Second, I also wish to thank my wife, Meriqua, for directing the production of this book. Thank you also to my daughter, Daniella, for typesetting the manuscript, putting the book together, helping with the proofreading, and also for writing the wonderful poem titled, "A Tribute to a Black Father Who Stayed" for this book; my son, Daniel IV, for designing the pages and for helping with the proofreading; my daughters: Danita, Danae`, and Daniqua, for designing the beautiful cover on this book and for doing great research in finding the quotes and Bible verses contained in this volume; and to my two youngest children, Danyel Ezekiel and Danyelle Elizabeth, for being good and quiet as I worked on this project.

I love you all and may God continue to bless you.

INTRODUCTION

"Honour thy father and thy mother: that thy days may be long upon the land which the LORD thy God giveth thee."
(Exodus 20:12)

There is a lot said, today, about black fathers not being responsible and staying with their children and taking care of their families. Well, this book is about honoring and paying tribute to those black fathers who, against the odds, have chosen to do the responsible thing and stay in the lives of their children. My father was one of those men.

This little book is a simple expression of appreciation and love for a good and loving father by the name of Daniel White Jr. Although he was not a perfect man, he made the decision to stay with his family no matter what and by doing so, he gave me the great benefits of his presence in my life, and of not making me a child of divorce. It is my hope that this statement does not offend those who grew up not knowing their natural father or not having the benefit of having him in the home. Even though I had a few holes in my soul that needed to be filled while growing up, thankfully, the painful hole that could have been caused by divorce was filled by a loving dad who did the responsible and right thing and who, quite frankly, put up with a lot of disrespect and foolishness to stay with his family.

I am also writing this book for the following three reasons:

1. To give God glory, praise, and honor for providing earthly dads for us and for being the ultimate Father.

2. To show honor and pay tribute to all the black fathers, both past and present, who stayed with their families and trained up their children in the way they should go. The black community is as strong as it is because of them.

3. To honor and pay tribute to the millions of good black mothers, such as my favorite aunt, Rebekah Credle of James City, North Carolina, who, by God's grace, after being divorced from an abusive husband, single-handedly successfully raised five boys, who all graduated from college. My hat is off to the millions of black mothers who, down

through the years, had to be the "mother and the father" to their children.

Ultimately, the aim of this book is to turn the hearts of all fathers—black, white, red, and yellow—to their children, and to encourage fathers to stay with the children they have and raise them for the glory of God.

—Daniel Whyte III
Dallas, TX

A Tribute to My Father's Life

CHAPTER 1

I decided not to make this book a biography of my father's life. I just want to give honor to my father for staying with his family and raising his four children. In this chapter, I will share with you some of the times that my dad and I spent together while growing up. But, let me first introduce you to my father.

My dad, Daniel White, Jr., was born in North Carolina in 1934. From what I understand, there was a difference of opinion about his birth date between my mother and my grandmother. But, my dad apparently leaned more to what my grandmother said his birth date was—1934. His early years were shaped during a pivotal time in history. The year he was born, Hitler became the leader of Nazi Germany. In 1939, World War II began, and it didn't end until 1945, when my dad was eleven years old.

During this time, the Jim Crow laws were still in place in the South. My grandparents protected him from the harsh realities of racism as best they could. My father was barely a grown man when the Civil Rights Movement got into full swing. He grew up during these changing times and, not surprisingly, he was affected by them. My father was barely thirty years old when John F. Kennedy was assassinated in 1963. He was in his early thirties when, in 1968, Martin Luther King, Jr. was shot in Tennessee and Robert F. Kennedy was killed two months later.

In this book, you will see that my father was characterized by a spirit of love and compassion for all people. He was optimistic about his own life and when his children came along, he was excited about the possibilities that lay before us. I believe that the events that shaped our world, and our country, during this time also helped to shape him into the man he was.

I was born in 1960 and I have some good memories of my dad, while growing up in Brooklyn, New York. I especially remember the fun times we had when he would take me with him to his jobs—especially to the mink fur coat company. I could sense how proud he was of me as his son as he introduced me to the Jewish owners. He would, every now and then, bring home pieces of mink fur for us children to play with. I also remember the times, as a little boy, sitting on my daddy's lap while he smoked his Kools cigarettes and let me sip on his Colt 45.

I also remember the times he took me with him to his

baseball practices. Back then, he was a semi-pro baseball player. I recall him hitting the ball and letting me run the bases for him. All of his teammates got a big kick out of that. Even though he was around his buddies, I did not feel left out; he made me feel like a part of them.

To this day, I still love my mother's cooking, and I wished that she was home more while growing up to do the cooking, but, to be honest, due to the fact that both my parents worked long hours, it was nothing for my dad to get in there and try to do something in the kitchen to feed his children. Now, my dad really thought he could cook. But, I, for one, endured his cooking because I knew it was going to be the same thing every time, regardless of the time of day. And what he cooked was something he called "cracklin pancakes." Now, "cracklin pancakes," which I have never heard of before or since, is basically some type of hard pork fatback which he would throw into the pancake mix and he would always serve it with some cheap, white, clear Karo syrup. Sometimes, he would fry some bologna to go with it, or something like that, but that was basically it. I ate it, but I wasn't too crazy about it. However, that was his way of loving his children and making sure his children ate, even though he was working two or three jobs.

As I look back on these times with my dad, they are funny now. Of course, when we were going through them, they didn't seem so funny. But, I can see the bigger picture now in that my dad really loved his children and he did the best he could with the background and knowledge he had to be the best father he could be.

However, not all memories of my father are warm, funny ones. I remember once I was asleep in my bedroom when I was awakened to screaming and arguing. With my new cowboy pajamas on and my little teddy bear in my hand, I got up and walked toward the noise, not knowing what to expect, and certainly not expecting what I saw. As I turned the corner, I saw my dad push my mother's head into the bathroom mirror and blood gushed out. At that time, I could not have been more than four or five years old. I did not know what was going on. All I knew was that I did not like what I saw. My parents separated for a while after that incident, and it was a very strange time not having my dad around.

By the grace of God, my parents got back together some time later, and I was very happy to have my father back in my life. Even though my parents didn't get along as well as they should have, my dad did not allow this to interfere with his love for his children. He enjoyed playing with us, taking us with him, and, of course, buying us snacks.

When I was about ten or eleven, I noticed a dramatic change in my dad's life. My dad truly became a born again Christian. This was not just a joining the church thing; it was not just a reformation. It was a transformation. This was the real deal and everything about my dad changed from that time in his life. He exemplified the love of Christ to everybody he met. Soon, God called him to preach the Gospel and his gift of singing started to shine through.

He did that for the glory of God for the rest of his life.

But, strangely, while he was making a positive change, I became more rebellious as a teenager and took a turn for the worse, and we started having serious problems in our relationship. One of the reasons we started having problems is because he became a popular preacher and Gospel singer in the area, and he also had a gospel television show which made things worse for me at school because I bore his name and everybody around town knew me as Rev. Daniel White Jr's son. That image made it difficult for me to be cool in school, and thus I had to work double to fit in with the in-crowd and not be seen as a square. You know what they say about preacher's kids.

Anyway, after I left home, I eventually became a Christian myself. My father and I soon developed a good father-son bond and relationship, which was a blessing. I cherish the times we spent together after that, even though they were few and far between. It was amazing how our lives mirrored each other in certain ways. I loved my dad very much and he loved me. After my father died and went on home to be with the Lord, I never shed one tear over his death because I had already made peace with him and I was very confident then and I am very confident now that I will see him again on the other side.

Even though we did not have a "Brady Bunch" family situation, and even though my dad and I had some problems in our relationship during my teenage years, I praise the Lord for the life of my dad and I thank God he stayed.

A Tribute to My Father's Love

CHAPTER 2

"Charity never faileth: but whether there be prophecies, they shall fail; whether there be tongues, they shall cease; whether there be knowledge, it shall vanish away."

—1 Corinthians 13:8

"Love is what it is."

—Daniel White Jr.

I can truly say that my dad was a loving man, and I believe that is the testimony of everyone who knew him. Not only did he have a special love for his children, but he loved all people and people loved him. I doubt very seriously if my dad had an enemy in this world.

My dad was not a very emotional man, but he expressed his love for me and my siblings in so many different ways.

I recall when I was about fifteen or sixteen years old and I was working to help shut down the county fair. When I did not show up at home by 1:30 AM, my dad got up out of his bed and came out to the fairgrounds to check on me and to see if I was okay. Surprisingly, he was not angry; he just told me that he was concerned, and that he could not sleep until he knew that I was alright. Even though I was trying to act cool in front of my friends, that really touched my heart.

At another time, I had gotten with a young lady, and to make a long story short, she became pregnant. She was one of the good church girls from a good family whose mother was a close friend of our family. I knew my father was very hurt over the matter, but instead of him getting on my case about it as he should have, as soon as we met up, he told me that he takes some responsibility because he felt like he had not been the father he should have been to me. Of course, I immediately and respectfully stopped him and told him that it was not his fault at all, but mine. However, that is the kind of love my father had for me and for his other children.

On another occasion, after my parents separated for a second time, right after my high school graduation, I went out on my own and started working as a restaurant trainer in other cities. When my dad found out that I was in South Carolina by myself at the age of seventeen, he would go out of his way to make special trips to see me and sometimes, he would stay with me for a while. Once, when he visited, even though he was a pretty well-known preacher in that region, and even though he did not drink beer anymore, I guess in an effort to connect with me, he bought a six-pack of my favorite beer (because he knew I drank), and at the same time, he brought me a Bible, with some verses he had selected for me to read. Now that I look back on it, it is kind of funny, but we sat there and drank some beer together and talked about the Bible and life. We had some of the best times of our relationship when he would make those trips to see me. Sometime later, after I had become a Christian, I wrote a letter to him telling him how much those trips meant to me. Afterward, he and my mother both told me that the letter I wrote, meant a great deal to him. And my dad not only showed this kind of love to me, but he showed it to my siblings as well as many other children in the community who did not have fathers. All the children in the community loved my dad and looked up to him as a father figure. He would call them "Boo-Boo" as he called us sometimes.

Yes, indeed, my dad exemplified the love of Christ to his children and to others, but to a certain extent, he sometimes loved us, including my dear mother, "too much." And he has admitted to this. You may ask how can he love "too much?" What I mean by that is my dear dad was probably never taught and never really understood that love meant sometimes saying "no" as well as sometimes saying "yes." Love, sometimes means, quite frankly, tearing a disobedient child's "ass" up when he is out of line. Love also means standing flat-footed and saying to your bossy wife, "Be quiet, I'll handle this." I am sure my dad did this sometimes, but the truth is, he didn't do it enough. As a result, bad things happened in our family that could have been prevented. For example, all four of his children practiced pre-marital sex and either got someone pregnant or got pregnant, thus bringing shame upon his ministry and upon his family. One of the biggest mistakes that my father made because of his big heart of love and his wanting everyone to be happy, is that he never took full reins of the leadership of our family. Quite frankly, my mother ran the show from the time that I can remember until my father's death and both of them have admitted as much. Consequently, when things are out of order like that, you get bad results.

Fathers, please stay with your family and show love to your family because they need you and your love. But, remember, to show the full spectrum of love. The Bible says that God, our Heavenly Father, *"is love,"* and He will pat you on the back when you do well, but He will also slap you on the behind when you do evil. The Bible says in Hebrews 12:6, ***"For whom the Lord loveth he chasteneth, and scourgeth every son whom he receiveth."*** Earthly fathers need to do the same. In fact, the Bible says in Proverbs 13:24, ***"He that spareth his rod hateth his son: but he that loveth him chasteneth him betimes."***

Dr. James Dobson once wrote a book titled, *Love Must Be Tough.* Fathers, in taking care of your responsibilities in your family, yes, have fun with your family and have many lite times together. There is nothing like those times on earth. In fact, it is a little bit of heaven on earth. But sometimes, as a father, your *love must be tough.*

1 Corinthians 13

Though I speak with the tongues of men and of angels, and have not charity, I am become as sounding brass, or a tinkling cymbal.

And though I have the gift of prophecy, and understand all mysteries, and all knowledge; and though I have all faith, so that I could remove mountains, and have not charity, I am nothing.

And though I bestow all my goods to feed the poor, and though I give my body to be burned, and have not charity, it profiteth me nothing.

Charity suffereth long, and is kind; charity envieth not; charity vaunteth not itself, is not puffed up,

Doth not behave itself unseemly, seeketh not her own, is not easily provoked, thinketh no evil;

Rejoiceth not in iniquity, but rejoiceth in the truth;

Beareth all things, believeth all things, hopeth all things, endureth all things.

Charity never faileth: but whether there be prophecies, they shall fail; whether there be tongues, they shall cease; whether there be knowledge, it shall vanish away.

For we know in part, and we prophesy in part. But when that which is perfect is come, then that which is in part shall be done away.

When I was a child, I spake as a child, I understood as a child, I thought as a child: but when I became a man, I put away childish things.

For now we see through a glass, darkly; but then face to face: now I know in part; but then shall I know even as also I am known.

And now abideth faith, hope, charity, these three; but the greatest of these is charity.

A Tribute to My Father's Legacy

CHAPTER 3

My dad's legacy is four-fold:

1. A legacy of true salvation and a changed life.

2. The uncanny ability to rise above average people and do extraordinary things without losing the common, down-home touch.

3. The contentment gene.

4. The knowledge of how to be a great father.

A Legacy of True Salvation and a Changed Life

I jokingly say sometimes, that outside of myself, I know of only one person in my family who truly got born again, and that person is my dad, Daniel White, Jr. I say that because when he accepted Jesus Christ as his Saviour his life changed dramatically. The Kools cigarettes that I mentioned earlier were gone, never to be seen again. Even though he drank a lite wine product every now and then, in moderation, the hard liquor days were never seen again. But the biggest proof of his true conversion to Christ was the fact that he showed genuine love to all people. It didn't matter who you were. My dad was not a respector of persons. He was incapable of treating a dignitary differently than he would treat a derelict. When he would drive, ever so slowly down the street, everyone got a wave, a honk of the horn, or a loud "alright now."

As you will see in the interview that I conducted across the kitchen table in his home, sometime before he died, my dad didn't attend his father's funeral, and interestingly, I didn't attend my father's funeral either. Neither have I ever shed a tear over my dad's death, because I knew that my dad was truly born again, and I have felt closer to him since his death than while he was living. I know for a fact that I will see him, face to face again, not too many days from now.

The Uncanny Ability to Rise Above Average People and Do Extraordinary Things Without Losing the Common, Down-Home Touch

"If you look behind you and nobody is following you, then you are not a leader."
—John Maxwell

My dad was a natural born leader, but, if you had met him, you would have never known he was a leader for these three reasons:

1. He never tried to be a leader.

2. He never pushed himself forward.

3. He never acted as though he was any different than the people who followed him.

Yet, when my father arrived on the scene, people looked to him as a leader, and people followed him because they knew he loved them with a genuine heart.

Before having Gospel shows on television was popular, particularly for black folk, my dad was on television every Sunday for years. Yet, when you saw him on the street, he was dressed in regular clothes, because he was also a janitor at the television station where his show was aired. And, unlike the preachers of today, he did not feel as though he had to drive a Cadillac or Lincoln to be somebody. He probably felt as though it would cause him to lose the common touch. This leads me to my next point.

The Contentment Gene

The third part of the legacy my dad left behind from his life is what I humorously oftentimes share with my wife and children, is something I call "the cheap gene." I am dubbing it here, for the book's sake, "the contentment gene," because my dad was not a cheap person, but what I am talking about here is my dad's penchant for and pleasure in those things that were not name brand and those things that were simple and/or old. He may have done some of this out of necessity, but I firmly believe that my dad got a secret thrill out of bringing home off brand sodas that just said "Cola" on the label. This is intriguing to me for two reasons: (1) my mother is the total opposite in that she loved the finer things of life and (2) the second reason is because this is one of the few things I have naturally taken after my dad. Thankfully, I can buy Charmin toilet paper for my family of nine if I wanted to, but like my dad, I get a secret thrill out of buying six rolls of toilet paper for $1.00 at Dollar General. I cannot explain why, but I enjoy getting things on the cheap like that. I guess I get the feeling I am getting over or something.

The Knowledge of How to Be a Great Father

Many people do not realize this, but God gives us parents so that we can learn from them in two ways—positively and negatively. The plan is, by doing so, a child can become a better person and a better parent, (because no parent is perfect) and thus raise up a better generation.

Even though I may not be great in every area of my life, my wife and children will tell you that I am a great father. I thank the Lord for that, but I owe my dad some credit as well. The reason is because I have learned from his life in a positive way and I have also learned from his life in a negative way. This is why it is important for a father to stay, even if he feels as though he is not being the best father he can be.

Positively: Like my dad, I really love my children. Not only did I learn this from my dad by his example, but this is also one of the few things that I naturally take after my father. I have a God-given love for my children, and because of that I have a great rapport with my children and always have since their birth. Of course, this is a gift from God.

Negatively: Unlike my dad, I learned negatively that love is to be expressed fully and balanced. In other words, love is to be expressed by a pat on the back when a child does well and a slap on the behind when a child does wrong.

As I briefly mentioned earlier, one of the mistakes my dad made was that he "loved us too much." He simply did not understand that love is expressed in many different ways. Because of this lack of understanding or maybe choosing not to accept this truth, he and my mother had constant marital problems because he would never rebuke her disrespect of him. I remember him saying to me on more than one occasion, "Danny, I do not want to say anything because I want to keep the peace." Well, I negatively learned from that that if a man can't say what he needs to say in his own house to have true peace, then he nor his family will have peace at all. Therefore, I practice the principle that, if there is not going to be any peace in the house because I have to say some things my wife or my teenagers do not like—let there be no peace. Fathers, you don't have real peace anyway, if you can't speak your piece. I have never subscribed to the idea that "if Mama ain't happy, ain't nobody happy." In my house, I know that if we don't all do what we are supposed to do the Bible way, ain't nobody going to be happy. King David said in Psalm 120:7: *"I am for peace, but when I speak, they are for war."*

Yes, we need to lovingly encourage our children with a pat on the back, and I do that all of the time, but we also need to lovingly give them a smack on the behind when they are disobedient. What has happened in our society, and particularly in the black community, is that black men have abdicated their role as disciplinarians of their children and have left it to the mothers. I am here to tell you that most mothers cannot chastise a boy like a man can. I must say here, as a credit to my mother and to so many other women, who knew the importance of chastisement, that they did the job that oftentimes the father should have done, of being the disciplinarian, and using corporal punishment to chastise the children.

Frankly, I cannot remember my dad cracking down on me other than one time when I was in the bathroom getting myself hooked up to go out to the club, and I was talking back to my dad about something we disagreed on regarding the use of one of the cars or something like that, and before I knew it, he broke down a locked bathroom door to get to me. And even then, he didn't hit me, but he sure did scare the hell out of me. Other than that, I do not

34

remember my dad whipping me or cracking down on me like my mother did. I am one of the millions who say: I wish my dad had given me more whippings. The truth is, I needed them. And folks, you know and I know that one of the reasons our children are acting as crazy as they are acting today, is because the father is not showing the full spectrum of love.

My father was not a perfect man, and he made some mistakes, but his legacy endures in the way he strived to live a good life, in the way he led and loved people, in what I learned from him about being content with the simple things of life, and in what I learned from him about how to be a great father.

A Tribute to a Black Father Who Stayed

by Daniella Whyte

My dad was loving, gentle and kind
        to my siblings and me.
In fact, he was kind to almost everyone
        he would see.

He didn't care for pomp or the expensive things
        He liked to get almost everything on the cheap.
My mother was the one who wanted all the bling
        But for my dad, fancy cars and such
                you could keep.

But one day, he met Jesus
        and his entire life turned around.
By his drinking, smoking, and other sins
        he was no longer bound.

At that point, he cared more about people
　　　　an encouraging word he would send.
To the church, Christ's work and service
　　　　this humble servant did lend.

Of course, he was not perfect
　　　　mistakes and failures he made.
But when he got to the end of his life
　　　　His joy and happiness did not fade.

　　　　His life, his love, his legacy he laid.
　　　This is a tribute to a black father who stayed.

Interview with My Father, Daniel White Jr.

CHAPTER 5

Special Note: *This is an informal interview that I did with my dad sometime before he died. I had never heard of anyone doing an interview with their father before. All I knew was that I was traveling in ministry a lot, and I had a family of my own at the time, and I knew when I interviewed him that that would probably be my last time seeing him alive. This interview was recorded by cassette tape, transcribed from the cassette tape and is virtually unedited. This interview was actually conducted at my dad and mom's house in Apalachicola, Florida. You will actually read the words of my dad about his life.*

Obviously, this interview is very significant to me personally. The significance of this interview for you, the reader, is that you are reading about a man's life whose father was born close to the time of slavery and certainly during the infamous Jim Crow period of our history here in America. Also, in this interview, you are witnessing three generations spanned—Daniel White Sr., Daniel White Jr., and Daniel White III. The picture that you see on the cover at the top represents three generations of Daniel Whites— my father, Daniel White Jr.; myself, Daniel White III; and my son, Daniel White IV. This picture was taken at our hotel room during my graduation from Bethany Divinity College and Seminary. This was a special occasion for my dad because he only had an eighth grade education and he was happy to see his son, who bore his name, break through the cycle and graduate, summa cum laude, with a Bachelor's degree in Theology.

If you and your dad are getting on up in age, I would encourage you to sit down and interview him so that you can pass it on to your children as well.

Here is the interview with my dad in his own words:

1. How old was grandpa (Daniel White Sr.) when he died?

I think he must have been close to 40. He must have been close to 40 years old because it seems as though he was 38 when I was born in 1934. My birth certificate states how old my father was and how old my mother was. He was somewhat older than my mother. I would imagine my daddy might have lived to reach maybe 42 before he died. So I am figuring my daddy, if he lived, might have been 90-92 years old. Because my mother she's like 86. I know he was at least 5 years older. In fact, my father could be just as old over my mother as I am over your mother. I believe it's almost 6 years; almost 7 years that I think that I am older than your mother...just like I am over...I don't know. It's a pattern. I don't know. It just seems like a pattern of some kind. My father, he worked at a mill. You know it was hard work.

2. Was that the mill across the river in James City, North Carolina?

Nearby where he worked. You know. Naturally, he would stop by just like I would stop by Toby if Toby lived near. He would stop by some evenings and then like it was in the old days—there was always a place—people could go by a certain house and relax. You know they probably wouldn't call it relax. But it was a place of refreshment that they go by and give them a little nip, and say, 'I'm tired. I deserve this,' and things like that. So I believe my daddy spent much time doing that.

You know I didn't know nothing about him being a ladies' man or anything like that. But those things he did. In other words, I didn't see him that way. There were many of us. By the time my father died, there were eight other children born. I was the seventh at that time. Seven or eight children at least because... Let me see: Dollie, Rebekah was also born. So I understood that I had lost a brother in the early years and he would have been named after one of your great-grandfathers or your great-great-grandfather.

You see your great-great-grandfather's name was Briss—

41

Briss White. That was your grand-daddy's father.

3. Briss White?

I think it's B-R-I-S-S or Bristol—B-R-I-S-T-O-L. But they call him Briss. That was your grand-daddy's father. And you know, while I'm there, your Uncle Toby has the oldest child named after your great-grandfather. He is the only one that has a son named Briss—after your grandfather's father. That's the only one that carry that name.

My father, like I said, he spent time, you know, like away from home like a lot of men back then; having not been taught; not that far away from slavery time. You know. Who was to teach him? You understand? And a lot of times men neglected their families. They didn't make much. They worked hard and they did whatever they could to find a little pleasure.

I don't remember my daddy putting me on his knee. But it seemed like to me that one time, one Christmas, while my father was living (I'm not even sure of this), it seemed like I got for that Christmas like a pair of blue overalls. Also maybe sort of a wooden toy or something like that which I deeply appreciated because this is the first time that I ever realized I received a toy of that nature. And kids didn't get no toy like that, you know, like they do today. My God! that one toy was like a miracle. You know that? I'm serious. It was like a miracle. And I can remember that.

Another thing—I think one of the much deeper memories

42

that I have—is that my father when he took sick, I was like a knee-baby. They called me a knee-baby or something like that. I don't know what that has to do with anything. I didn't understand it. But I know I remember I had two other sisters—Rebekah and Dollie. But it seemed like I used to be around my daddy's sickness in the old house where my father...where we lived...two-story house. And...

4. That's the house that used to be out front on Scott Street in James City, North Carolina, right?

Right out front. And you came to it when you was a child along with your Uncle James and I, and the house was still there—before the new house was built. And I remember that my father lived...his bedroom...his bedroom... They stayed upstairs in the house and grandfather lived downstairs. He stayed upstairs in a front bedroom and Mama used to iron and everything up there. While he was sick, I used to be around quite a bit. But I don't know if at that time he was well enough to do any talking to me or anything like that. But I do believe I used to be in that room playing on the floor or something like that. You know, I think I was big enough, but I don't think I would get away from home too far at that time when my father was sick. It seemed as though when he passed...when he passed...I believe it was 1942. The first few months of 1942 it seemed like to me. I didn't go to the funeral. I don't think they would let me go to the funeral. I don't know whether it had affected me or not.

43

5. You were named after him?

Yeah. I was not the first boy, but I was the one named after my daddy. I don't believe he had a middle name. I think his name was Daniel White and I was Daniel White, Jr. And I am told I look much like him. When you see me, you see my father. Sort of what Jesus said, isn't it? If you seen me, you seen the Father.

6. Yes, well, that's interesting because you really don't look that much like Mother Tempie. So it has to come from the other side.

I'm told that my sister Nancy, who's passed on, and my sister Hattie and I are the ones that look more like my daddy. My daddy was on the darker side; more like my complexion. You know like I said that time, I can vaguely remember that. I don't remember much activities because like I said he took sick and to me it's in the early years. And as I said, they did not let me go to the funeral for some reason or another.

I was young. I remember I stayed and I looked out of the window across to Mt. Shiloh Missionary Baptist Church. And you know, you can see it from any window outside. And that was long ago—50 years ago. And I know I felt something. I didn't understand. But I know I felt something. It was my first encounter with death. You know, I didn't understand it. And at the time, I supposed I missed him to whatever degree it could have been. But it was those two ladies...I think my grandfather could have

44

still been living. I think he died a little later. But he also took sick. I didn't want to get to that yet. But he also took sick from an accident or something like that. My father, I never really got to know him like some kids do—unfortunately. It's the kind of relationship I think you could miss. I'm sure that I missed it and realized it. God is just as good to me. He let me realize the impact of it because that was somebody to love me and to nourish me.

7. But, Daddy, you have a tremendous relationship with your mother even though she had several children. How was it growing up after that, after your daddy passed? And what do you remember during those days?

My mother began to work; day work they called it at that time. It's maid work. She began...I don't know the first people she worked for. But I know [it was] thirty something odd years ago. I can remember at least thirty years ago she began to work for a family by the name of Capers. She might have worked for their parents at that time. So...better than thirty years ago, more like forty years ago 'cause I worked for the same Capers more than forty years ago. I believe I was just twelve. So you see, that's got to be more than forty years ago. More like forty-five years ago.

My mother, she worked in those people's houses and took care of us along with the help of my grandmother. And my mother, you know...it was a small income, but we were able to survive. It's amazing. I tell you, it's amazing to think you never went hungry even though it wasn't a lot of money. But my mother worked out...she worked out at the homes there until I believe the Lord opened up a door for her to go somewhere, where she could make more money. And as she went away to work and make money, Mama Lou, Grandma Lou, we called her Mama Lou, she took care of us. She was the mother and father for us while my mother worked out.

8. O.K. I remember the name Mama Lou...

Well, you were about three years old before she died. You had seen her—Mama Lou—when you came home first as a child. That time Mama Lou was not doing too well. She was about 81 when you first saw her.

9. Was she Mother's natural mother?

No. Same thing. She married my mother's father. Now what happened...

10. Oh, O.K.

That's what happened. You see, it seems as though she was a stepmother to my mother. And I don't know for sure, but it seemed as though Mama Lou was married in the family. And it seems like she married my mother's father because he was a widow, too. At least she was a widow and she married him. That made her become my mother's stepmother. But so far as a maternal grandmother, blood-wise she couldn't have been better. Even today, Ms. Anne Gaddis who is a historian in the James City area tells you

Mama Lou couldn't have been any better if she had birthed us in the world because that's the way she took care of us while my mother worked out and worked in different places such as Miami. Mama was down in Miami before Miami was built up and as corrupt as it is today, you know. And the money was better, you know. She was able to do more for us than she would if she stayed right home.

11. So when you say "worked out" that means that...

Worked out from the house.

12. She stayed out a number of years all in a period of time?

A number of years. All in a period of time. For years she would go out and work and send the money home. She did that when Miami was building up.

13. Daddy, actually you didn't have too much time with your mother while you were growing up, did you?

Well, O.K. I see what you mean. When my mother was around I had a good relationship with my mother. And then you got to understand, when my mother came back home to settle down I was around a while. My mother was away when I went in the Air Force. She was living and working in Virginia. Now, to my knowledge, my mother got married again. She married a man by the name of Jesse Kennedy. They moved from Virginia and came home to

47

live there at the house.

So let's see...I don't remember exactly what year it was, but I believe it was...I was a young kid. I don't remember..It might have been...I was still a teenager. I think they might have come home in the 50's or 60's or something like that...to live. It seemed like to me...I don't remember whether I was in the Air Force or not. It's kind of clouded up to me. But I know she supposedly had gotten married again to this Mr. Kennedy—Jesse Kennedy.

And they came home to live anyway. And after a while when he got around New Bern and start learning the ways and the people [he] started fooling around. To me, my mother, still that was not her lifestyle. Mama was not a woman that liked to go out. She, as long as I can remember, I never knew my mother going to any night club or joint. I don't know what she did when she was living in Virginia or what not. But my mother never got into drinking to my knowledge, or smoking 'cause she just had high moral standards. I just don't believe, you know. But anyway, when she was around the home and I wasn't away from home myself, when I left to go in the Air Force in 1952 my mother was working out in Virginia. Grandmother was still taking care of us and Mama came back home, I believe, while I was away.

Shortly after I was away, that time my being in the Air Force, the Lord blessed me so that I was able to send a little money home to help out. So my mother was able to stay home. She and my grandmother continued to take care of the business together. Then I would come home and spend that time with them. To tell you the truth my adult life I was already married before I could spend as much time with my mother. I was already in my 20's. To tell you the truth, I came home from New York and settled down and spent those nine years in the James City area. But until that time, those were the only adult years that I spent for any account of time. So I was around Mother Tempie then. You know that might have had a lot to do with the fact that when I decided to leave and to come here that was again missing time. But the time that I had around her, I can remember this as though it was yesterday. That was something that my mother used to do when I was around and I myself do the same thing with Raevyn. My mother had a habit when I was around, you know, if I slept or what not, she used to play with my kneecap. To me that was a sign of love. To me it was. It was time—the best that I could understand quality time. And I remember that wasn't too far before I grew up. I could remember sitting around when my father was sick. I might have been young enough one time. I stayed with Mama and she used to play with my kneecap. I remember that so well. That May...May would have been before she left home.

14. Daddy, Mother Tempie has long black hair and has high cheekbones. Could you share with me about our Indian heritage?

I am told that my mother's mother grandmother was an Indian.

49

15. Full-blooded?

She could very well be full-blooded Indian and I am told she could sit on her hair. Her hair was so long. I may be wrong, but it seems to me that she was a very powerful, healthy lady. You know—her size. I am told this. And it seems that I can remember that more than anything— the distinguished length of her hair. She could sit on her hair. And so I believe that's where my mother got her long hair from. You noticed about my mother's hair, even at 86 years old, her hair is less gray than mine, and she still has that good grade of hair.

16. Now, Dad, I know that you have a good relationship with all kinds of people—white, etc., but do you recall growing up with any racial problems? Did you ever have any problems with racism? Did your Dad ever have any problems with racism? Did your Mom ever have any problems with racism?

I tell you, now, I really don't remember anything about my daddy having any kinds of problem. I just imagined the hard labor that I mentioned, working on the strawboard or something like that; whatever the boss wanted. I think at that time if a man kept his nose clean and worked he had less racial problems because of a "Yes, Sir" / "No, Sir" thing. So, I think that eliminated the problem. Even if a man was ten years your junior, you still had to respect him because he was white. And at that time you didn't contest that. You understand what I'm saying? Because of his color.

Because of his position. And I don't know if my Daddy ever had any kinds of problem. I never heard of anything like that.

17. How about yourself?

Well, I personally...Let me put it this way. My mother, as I may have mentioned, working out at the white people's house in New Bern in an area called The Gent. She worked for the Capers. Like I said, I don't know if they are the first people she worked for. They were very, very good to my mother so far as racial, you know. And they thought of her as a part of the family. But there was something about your grandmother, Mother Tempie, that she did not (and I mean this) take junk from anybody—color or anything. There was something about her. She was very gifted. My mother, your grandmother, she was a very smart woman and a very particular woman—articulate; very articulate, even today.

18. She was very proud in a good sense?

In a good sense. Right.

19. Dignified?

Dignified. That's a good word. Because she didn't allow people to say anything to her. I don't care what color they were. So, I'm thinking that my mother had very little trouble because she stood up for herself and this didn't make no difference who it was. There was times when she had to stand up against blacks as well as whites. It was sort of like since my father had died at an early age, that people in the community seemed to think that you're so poverty-stricken. We were very proud people then, you know—which is known today. We were very proud people in our family.

My mother (I don't know if she had gotten anything), one incident that comes to mind over forty years ago. My mother was in McClennon's Department Store and white salesperson at that time they had a tendency to follow around black people; thought that they could dictate to you what to buy. And I do remember this distinctly, the lady tried to tell my mother something like this: "This would be good for you." I remember my mother's reply as if it were today. She said, "I know what I want. I know what I want. Don't tell me." She said it. She said it. She said it. And I am talking well over forty years ago. This was in McClennon's Department Store. And I do remember another incident while shopping at an early age for Hattie and myself. Your Aunt Hattie, she had a quick mouth and my mother was buying, probably for Easter or something like that; something Hattie didn't want. Mother Tempie thought it would be okay; something about a pair of shoes in Mary's Shoes Store. I remember that. And Hattie disagreed about the shoes and she wanted some other type shoes, and I remember your grandmother taking Hattie by the ear and bringing her out of the store and I'll tell you today, your Aunt Hattie remembers it too. It did not make any difference where you were. She didn't lose her composure. She did what she had to do.

20. So Mother Tempie had a positive influence on your life?

My mother had a positive influence. Do you know what? I think a lot of what happened to my mother about white people—they have always been exceptionally good to Mother Tempie. And I found that God has blessed me to deal with white people in the same way. I sincerely mean that. You know you wonder some things are hereditary so to speak. My mother had a great rapport, a great relationship with people that she worked for. They didn't take her as an employee, so to speak, as much as they took her as a part of the family. And I've been involved into people's lives that I worked for. I was treated like family down through the years. And I'm talking about when I first even met your mother, I had people that were Jewish people, even when you were born, that were like family and they treated me like family.

21. Was this in New York?

This was in New York.

22. I remember that because I remember one time that you took me up to see one of your Jewish friends.

I most certainly did.

23. I think you kind of had a little job with him.

53

I worked for [them] in the fur market. I worked in the fur market.

24. I remember those little mink furs you used to bring home.

That's right. Mr. Irvin Leesack, he was like a father to me, and you were the first-born. And he did things [for me]. I mean they just bought new things for you. O my God! I had to take you back to the fur market area and then the factory where we worked. I also took your mother. And by this time I think your mother may have been taking Sheila too; either carrying Sheila or Sheila was born. But I think you were walking.

25. I don't know, but that might have had something to do with my tremendous love and appreciation and respect for the Jewish race today.

Perhaps.

26. We have a paper that reaches the African-American community, but we always have something in there about Jews, you know.

It would be very difficult for me to forget the Jewish people that was in my life. And that began in 1958. It was really...I think I began to get a new education when I started to work in New York City. I did not know anything about Jewish people before I went there. All I knew were the Blacks and the Whites. That's all I knew. But God had blessed me.

I think I missed something out when I was talking about your Mother Tempie about how she had that independence, that dignity and all. I worked for this man that my mother worked for who owned a bakery. That's who Toby worked for. I worked for them also. My sisters did certain things for this family. This family seemed to have been put in our lives so that we could make it—the Capers. I shall never forget them. Mr. Alfred Capers, Jr. They called him 'Shorty' Capers. He was a good man. He may have had some prejudice. But you see, I didn't know anything about that. I didn't even understand that. You see, the one thing about it at that time was, there was no need for white people to show a whole lot of prejudice because there was no uprising at the time. So he treated me well, too. In other words, by working at this location, I never had to go on anybody's farm. All the jobs that I had was in buildings. From an early age, like twelve years old, I began to work in buildings.

Like I said, it had to be the Lord because academically, whatever I learned in school wasn't about what I worked at. I worked in a bakery factory. I may have known "the butcher, the baker, the candlestick maker." But I knew nothing about baking. And I was given an opportunity as an all-around person because they taught me, and I was able to learn. That was in the bakery shop.

27. Was this in New York or North Carolina?

This was in North Carolina. I jumped at that because of my mother. A lot of the things that happened to my mother had a lot to do with my coming up because the people that she worked for also gave us jobs. The parent of the Capers that my mother worked for, I also worked for them too. I also grew up playing with Mr. Capers, my mother's boss. I grew up playing with his daughter. She was like a tom-boy. And she had all of the baseball equipment and stuff that a boy would have. We didn't even know the difference. We didn't understand about black and white. You know? We didn't even understand that. Her daddy had a piece of land near where they lived—the clearing. The clearing area. And we used to play out there. We played baseball at that time. So all this was before I went to New York. This was before I went into the Air Force.

28. How long did you work in the bakery?

I started working there...I was big enough to work there from elementary school and a little while afterwards. I would go in the mornings and they would bring me back to go to school. But all of that was before I went to New York; before I went into the Air Force. I almost missed that because it's quite important. I grew up there. You had asked me about racial encounters, and I had not really encountered any great racial pressures.

29. Now, Daddy, you have how many brothers?

Right now, I have two brothers living. It was four boys up until like '68. My oldest brother, James, died. Four brothers and six sisters. It was still ten of us up until '68.

30. What were their names from the top-down?

The oldest brother was your Uncle James Alpert. The next one would be your Uncle William. He's in Virginia today. Now actually, Nancy on my father's side, I believe she's a little bit older than James. It would have been Nancy, James, William, Louise, Toby, Hattie, me, Dollie Mae, Rebekah, and the one that never saw father, Cherry. She never saw father. He died while Mama was carrying her.

31. So, it's nine then?

Nine.

32. And in growing up because grand-daddy wasn't there and mother had to work, did you all grow up closer? Because you have a close relationship with all of them.

That's the truth. Sometimes you're not able to explain the gift of God. Not really. Because it has to be a gift of God to have an established relationship with your family and when you weren't taught step by step necessarily but at the same time you didn't see no hatred either. In other words, you saw people doing the best that they could with what they had to do it with. We just grew up with a good relationship. I don't know what problems any of my brothers and sisters may have had with any other part of the family. All I know is that I don't have any problems

57

with any of my sisters and brothers. So that's the Lord again. I have a great relationship with my sisters and brothers.

33. With all of them?

And with nieces and nephews. I don't know how to explain that. It's the love of God.

34. So after you worked at the bakery, how old were you when you left?

I guess I might have worked there 'till I was 14-15, then I began to work in construction. I think I may have mentioned that. I started working with a construction company out of South Carolina after that in my off time.

35. You worked there how long?

It may have been a year, a couple of years—coming out of school and joining the service. So, it might have been a year, a year and a half or two. You needed that time to fulfill your life so it could have been longer. You know what I mean. I loved what I did working in construction. You were out there many hours as a teenager, and I guess that's where my love for carpentry came in. I used to be a petition man. Once the foundation was laid, I was with what they called the petition crew. Really, I loved it. I loved it. They would use chalkline to lay out from the blueprints the section on top of that slab floor. And I really loved it.

36. So is that pretty much where you learned how to do carpentry work?

Well, it had to be that. Along with it being a gift of God. You see, my grandfather, Tobias; my grandfather on my Mother Tempie's side, that was her father. He was a self-made type carpenter. I don't know about any schooling, but he was the man in town that helped people with fallen houses. There was no job too tough for him. If it needed straightening up, if it was leaning, Grandpa Tobias could lean it up again. Sometimes a storm would come and lean people's houses. They had to lean it up against posts. Somehow, he was a very powerful man. My Grandfather Tobias was the first man that I heard about being double-trained. Had something to do with his wrist. He was a very powerful man. He worked a lot by himself.

37. So you remember that about him?

I remember that. I remember when he...that's why I said he died after my father because one time it seemed as though I stuck a splinter in my knee and I can imagine this is like over fifty years ago. Seemed like yesterday. I can see it, how that he got the splinter out of my knee. What had happened, it had stayed in there and hurt me. The knee had swollen up and it had got infected. And my grandfather, the same man got it out with a needle of some sort, and opened it up and let the pus run out. My grandfather, the same one, he was a carpenter. Seems as though he burnt a needle or something. I don't know how he did it. I remember him. See, my grandfather got hurt.

He used to be a ship builder too. He used to build ships—masts for ships and stuff like that. And it seems as though on one job a rusted nail stuck him in the leg, and he neglected to go and have anything done about it. I remember that. I remember that. So quite a while he suffered that. But I did have that encounter with my grandfather, my mother's father.

38. Okay. How long were you at the bakery?

I would say three years because I was growing up and still going even from school. So at least three years I was in the bakery business.

39. All together, how long did you go to school?

Let's see. A total of nine years. Afterwards I tried to get back into school and other ways through the college media. I went to school in the Air Force. To me going back to school there I learned a lot more about skills. But you know somehow or other, in order to pass the test to get into the Air Force, I had to have some kind of gift because things that I had never seen I had to identify and pass in order to get into the Air Force. It was at that time not an easy branch to get into. The Army was the easiest branch because you could be almost a moron to go into the Army. At that time, many guys could hardly spell their names went into the Army.

40. So after the grade school years, you had a varied education experience through the Air Force and the

GI Bill? Did you go to J.T. Barber High School?

Oh, no, they did not have anything after school. Do you mean in the early years? That was West Street High School. That was the high school that I went to.

41. You went to James City Elementary, right?

James City Elementary and West Street High School. And also, Danny, like I said, I went to school in the Air Force. But I also got hooked up with another school where I was stationed at. I was stationed at Port O'Connor, Texas, and I made friends in a place called Port Arthur, Texas. There were those that befriended me at a school there. I think the name was Adam School—Adam High School or something like that, I think; named after one of the former principals. I got a little something there too and after coming out of the Service under the GI Bill, I went and got some more academics. You see, what I am saying, even though it was a trade school, I went to Craven Community College. Then I transferred and went to Lonoa Community. By this time, I was working at the television station. I had already gotten a good break then.

42. When you left high school, what led you into the Air Force? How did that come about?

Okay. After I came out of school, I worked. I was like in the tenth grade, but I worked. I started working. But you know, it's a funny thing about working—when you start making that money you don't see the need to go to school then. And like I said, I believe I was a very gifted person. I was able to catch on. I was strong, but I wasn't dumb. I don't think I was dumb because I was able to do pretty smart things. I know it was the gift of God because all my baseball time I was in there too. See, from the time I worked for the Capers from twelve years old up...I married in the '60s, the '70s was before I really quit my baseball thing.

43. You were heavily involved in baseball?

Very! Very much! I loved it better than I did eating. I loved it better than I did anything. But you were saying about what led me to the Air Force. [I was] working and there was a friend of mine, he and I worked, and we got to talking one day. We said we wanted to do something better and so one day we decided to go to the recruiting office. We went down to the recruiting office and this friend of mine (He's dead. He's been dead now several years), his name was Clem Ford. We went and took the test. Both of us passed. We went about our business and went back to work. We would have work sometimes and the job wasn't there sometimes. One day we got a phone call. In fact, at that time I am not sure whether or not we had a phone. They called from the recruiting office and said the quota that they needed was filled. We must have waited a good while to be part of that quota. They called for us and in a short time we were getting processed to go. Like one day and almost the next day we were on our way to Raleigh. And at the same time my Grandmother Lou was taking care of us. It was a sad day now. We had to leave her. But it was a good thing.

44. You were about 17 then?

I was 17 going about six months or so to be 18.

45. So what kind of experience was that for you to go to Raleigh, catch a plane going to Lackland Air Force Base, doing basic training and then the Air Force experience?

Being young and wanting something to happen in my life, it was a [thrill] I never planned for. I never understood it. I didn't know what was happening. It was happening so fast. All I know was that I wanted it better. I wanted it better. And I wasn't doing all that bad because at this time I had my first car already. I was seventeen years old with my first car and thinking that I was poor. But you don't have your first car at seventeen in 1951 and be poor. Although I may not have had as much as some other kids, but other kids didn't have no car either, and was working. I also missed out the fact that I was working from about fifteen to seventeen outside of Cherry Point. I was working for the Mezingos Restaurant. That's where I also bought my car because he was into selling cars, too. And I bought my first car at that time.

I bought my first car in 1952 and when I left to go into the Air Force I had to leave my car with somebody. I thought I could trust a guy that I knew. We played baseball together. We were very close. You know I love baseball so naturally I became attached to him and so I left my car with him. I lost the car. That was an experience.

But I went on to the Air Force. And you asked me what kind of experience that was. It was the greatest experience of my life. It was the plateau of my life that began. That was really the beginning of my growing up. Even then you said something about all things working for your good. But even at that time although I didn't understand it, it was the beginning of coming into maturity. That was some experience. I mean one day I'm around trying to figure out when I'm going to play ball or whatever I was going to do, and I get the phone call and in 48 hours or less my whole life changed. I'm on a plane that evening. That was so exciting. I never saw a more beautiful sight in my life.

46. That was an exhilarating feeling.

It's hard to explain it, Danny, because I didn't know fear. That was before I knew fear. In the clouds. In the clouds, man. That was the most beautiful sight you ever see. It was in the evening when I was flying, and we reached the place so many, many miles away from home.

47. So how long did basic training last for you?

Eight weeks

48. You went through that pretty good?

I went through that very good. I made good friends with the practical instructors. I was singing. I didn't think I would be singing then because I kept out of the church—Mount Shiloh. I was singing in Mount Shiloh's choir from an early age. I was singing and I kind of made friends with the Assistant T.I.—the Technical Instructor. I kind of made friends with them. Before I left basic training, I really hit it off good with the Sargeant and Corporal Mueller. Mueller was a German, but he was [nice]. I liked that guy. I used to mock him.

49. Did you have a lot of guys in your troop?

Well, I tell you, it seemed as though I hit it off with quite a few of them.

50. Was it mixed back then?

O yeah. O yeah. A good [number of] blacks in there. But somehow or another the Lord allowed me to find faith in people even at an early age. I had a guy (was a friend of mine) that was Polish. But out of all the blacks and some whites, I was the only one that could pronounce his name better than anybody. So that had to be a gift. Then it goes to my mother—a very articulate lady even today. I remember that. I'm talking about 1952. I could pronounce his name better than anybody there. There were some of them in the Air Force then, they were a bunch of farmers. [They] had no business being in there. They walked like farmers. And there were some whites that need to be home with Mama 'cause they were too young. But I went on—went on in the Air Force to get stable.

51. What kind of training did you do? What did you train in?

I got out of basic training and was going to school in a teaching job. It's in academics and aptitude tests. What you're best qualified for. My field was in electronics. I worked out of the electrical department. I worked with civilian workers. And do you know what? A tall, white man named Snydor, he was the one I liked best of all the civilians. There was another head man. He was kind of tough. He might have been prejudiced or what not. I try to give nobody reason to give me a hard time. I try to do what I have to do. You can call it what you want, but I did what I had to do. I can't remember the name of this other head man over Snydor. But Snydor was the one I liked best.

So I was in the electrical department and I worked close with the civilian people. I was in what they called the Air Installation Squadron. We did a lot of electrical work. And as the years go by I liked it. All I had to do...I was the trouble shooter. I used to go out riding the truck. I used to go out two or three times a night and check the base. That was the kind of position that I had.

52. How long did you stay in?

I stayed in the basic squadron all of my years in the service.

53. How long was the training?

It was the OJT. You worked on that field the whole time you were in the service.

54. It was different from when I was in the Air Force. We had our basic training first, and then they shipped us off to another base for training.

I was quite fortunate because they shipped me from San Antonio then they send you to a different squadron and whatever you call that—orientation or something like that. Then they send you to the department that your academic scores and aptitude test show that you qualify for. At least I didn't have to go into construction. At least I was able to work at that particular location whether my mark was three or six. The Lord just blessed.

55. Even today it's hard to get in the electronics field.

Oh, yeah. But I didn't know then, Danny, that I should follow it up. I still know some electrical stuff from my experience. Some people that I know today that are friends of mine are in electrical work. I just didn't apply myself to that experience. I should have.

56. Of course, the Lord would have to lead you in that direction.

Oh, yeah. I can do some of all of it today to the extent that I can carry it to the point where I can hook it up. But I just trust somebody else. I wired a lot of places but the main line some one had to wire it for me. But even if you did it and something happened they had some papers to prove you did it wrong. And if you end up in court, and if you did it and something went wrong, you can get in a world of trouble.

57. How long did you actually stay in the Air Force?

Three years and nine months.

58. Three years and nine months. Almost four years.

Because if you wanted to come out and go to school… When I went to school, I made more money going to school than I did when I was in the Air Force. I was making $315.00 extra a month and I was working two or three jobs then.

59. Were you playing baseball all throughout the Air Force?

I played baseball pretty off and on throughout the Air Force. I played baseball for the Air Force. I also played for civilian teams in the cities. I played for a black outfit out of Austin, Texas, in the city. That was the Austin Indians. And I also played with another team. This was a Hispanic team. I don't think it was but two blacks on the team. I can't remember the name of the team right now.

60. Was this down in Texas?

This was also in Texas. I pride myself on knowing enough about baseball that I could get a job. I guess you might call it the evangelist baseball player because, not that I was preaching, but I could get into the hustle of any other job about anywhere, you know. The evangelist, he had to go from place to place and use his skills. And I was able to use those skills that I had to play to get jobs on different teams. I was playing with the Air Force when I didn't have a game scheduled. Hardly would we ever play on weekends. We played some weekends. I had time off. I had a regular job. You know, like a five day a week job. Then I got hurt. After I got hurt then...I got a little gun-shy while playing ball. Although I [continued to] play ball even though I was hurt.

61. How did you get hurt?

I got hurt in 1953. I'd come home and I went back and I was playing softball with the squadron; not the base team. I was playing squadron baseball—softball, rather. And I was playing shortstop then too. What was called a Texas Leaker is a ball that looks like it is too short for the outfield and too deep for the infield. I ran out to get the ball and I caught the ball. But a guy that was playing left field or center field ran into me. And when you're running and not looking—see I was running out and this guy was coming in, and he was as hard as a rock. This man was in exceptional physical condition. He broke my tibia in about three places. However, I never dropped the ball.

I spent some five months in the hospital. I think it was the latter part of that year when I got out—like July 20, 1953. Sometime in July. I had gone back home on furlough. I spent the latter five months in the hospital because of the nature of the break. You know, I got a little skeptical.

But still played ball after I got well because I always favored in that league. That's what messed me up. I really thought I would make a major league player. That's all I could think about. I didn't care about any career in the Air Force. And I thought that I would play even after I got married.

62. Didn't you play for a semi-pro team?

The Nationals. This was the Brooklyn Nationals. We played against other semi-pro teams as well. We went to West Virginia and we played against at that time it seems like the Cincinnati Reds. Or some guys that were on this team were gonna go and play for them. That was an experience. We traveled so far. What happened, they had a homeboy, but the homeboy was already shot by the time. You know he had already been out there a long while playing ball. By that time he was about burnt-out by the time I met him. But they were trying to feature him as a pitcher for their team because we all were going for Brooklyn.

This guy named Snooky; a good friend of ours. His name was Snooky Evans and he lived, of course, with your grandmother when she lived on Tompkins Avenue. He was the manager so naturally when we all got home to West Virginia the team was competing up there. They let the homeboy pitch. When the homeboy pitched, it was like throwing little eggs at them. And them fellows liked to kill us.

Then I was pitching, too, at this time. By this time, I had really settled down as a pitcher then. I could do anything.

70

But I had settled down as a pitcher. I realized I had a real good arm; a couple of good pitches. And so, after the game I was like out on lease, they called me in to relieve this guy. And I could have stopped. I think the guy hit one home-run off me. He hit it off me and that tied. We were somewhere about six to five. And after that I settled down and held them. That was an experience for me.

63. Were you in Virginia when you flew in your first Air Force plane?

Yes, that's when I was in West Virginia. Now that was scary. I had never seen them mountains before. Look like you're going to run right into the mountains but you go around them. That was another experience.

64. After the Air Force experience, how did you meet mom?

Let's see. Your Uncle James came to James City, North Carolina, after he and his wife got separated, or something or another. It was serious. And he had traveled without sleep to try to locate his wife to South Carolina from which she had come from originally. He was harshly received there by some of the in-laws. And he just didn't know where she was. He had traveled all the way from New York without sleep, had not been able to rest, plus he didn't know what had happened to his wife.

One day he came and all the funds were gone. So I've been home from the Air Force since July 20, 1956. And this was happening like between the very first of January 1957 and the second of January. He came home and he was in bad shape. And somehow or another, I don't know...

65. That thing really got to him?

Yes, it got to him. It got to him—heartbreak. He asked me was I going back with him. I didn't plan to go to New York. Any way I went with him. I went with James and one of the very first things I did, this was like Wednesday and I think I was on a truck working with friends of James like the next day. I met with him and worked with him a while at different things, and I joined this church.

Well, I went to the church that very first Sunday and saw your grandmother—Mother Beaman. I met her that Sunday. That first Sunday in Brooklyn, New York, St. Paul's Disciple Church I met her mother.

66. Now, was this St Paul's on Tompkins Avenue?

That was on Gates and Tompkins Avenue. I did know she was going to be my mother-in-law 'cause she was singing with the Gospel Chorus and I was the feature soloist on the Gospel Choir.

67. How did that come about so quickly?

Well, I met some guys through my brother James going to that church and they knew about me. And Toby, your Uncle Toby, had previously been in that church. He had gone overseas. Toby went in the Army. He went in the Army and had gone overseas. He left that vacancy there and I just happened to come along at that time to pick up that spot where Toby left off.

After having Toby and then learning that I could sing a little bit I think your Uncle Toby might have promoted that. The very first Sunday that I was there I sang. I made a pretty good impression upon the people. And so I stayed on. Until I left there I was still singing. So that was 1957-1958. I was singing. So that's how that started there. As the years went by, in 1959 I met your mother.

68. Where was it that you met her?

At the church. It was the beginning of something that was gonna be bigger than me. The boys say, you know when it happen. So obviously I must have known when it happened. I had to give it up. I'll never forget that. And I met Mommy there. We got married in '60. So that was inevitable. I met her there at St. Paul's Disciple Church and we worked in the choir. We sang in the choir a while. And we started courting and things like that. The funny thing about it, I guess it was the way that I got to know her—Gunsmoke. That was my favorite show. I just told her that I wanted to see Gunsmoke. She invited me to come there to her mother's house to see Gunsmoke. I don't know. It was something—a magnetism, because sometimes you can't even explain how you go somewhere and meet somebody and don't want to leave. How in the world that happen? I didn't want to leave. I tell you. And so we just got tied up and had it going strong; very, very close and everything happened so fast and then we got married.

69. How long did you all go together before you got married?

About eight months we knew...I think it's something, Danny, that you know. And I've heard it said even by her that either you know or you don't know because you will never know all there is to know about a person, and you don't even need to know. But you know one thing—you'll be knowing that you want to get married. I don't know. It's something that happens. When it's time for you to do a certain thing, when that time is right, boom! And that's what happened to me. I know. I'm still married to the woman that I am, after thirty-two years. Thirty-two years. Somebody said it couldn't be done. Thirty-two years.

70. Now, I remember a little bit about St. Paul's.

St. Paul's gave me an opportunity to develop my singing skills without me really understanding it. I probably didn't even realize that I had the ability and I didn't know anything about anointing. But somehow or another there were people pushing and encouraging me into singing and it helped my talent to materialize in St. Paul. And then, I was highly influenced by the pastor—Bishop Johnson. There was a lot of things I learned from that old man— the way he preached, the way he talked and didn't talk down from anybody. I learned a lot from him. He was a tough man. He was a tough preacher. Sometimes he said a lot of things to hurt your feelings. Sometimes I didn't know whether he was talking about me or what. But he really helped me.

71. So he had a positive influence?

Yes. He had a positive influence. Perhaps my situation today in the ministry was enhanced by his showing me how not to do certain things. Okay, I didn't think that if you love people you were to be verbally abusive. But a lot of time you lose yourself when people are constantly bringing you problems and you can't handle that all the time. You start fighting back self. You don't let the Lord fight your battle. You fight it yourself. I believe that's what happened. But you learn how not to do certain things.

72. Now the children started to come. What kind of impact did we have on your life? Married, have children coming, what did it mean to you? A lot of black men didn't stay around?

With me, Danny, I would say it was the Lord. In fact, the Lord knew better than I that that's what I needed to become the man that I would need to be. The Lord know I needed that in my life to make me pray. You know I really believe that. God knows best. I don't know what would have happened to me. I probably would have been dead in the graveyard had it not been that the Lord put Shirley in my life—my wife in my life and children in our lives. We were destined to be some kind of example and I think we've tried to do that, even today.

She and I talk sometimes now and we say there was nobody teaching us anything. So it had to be the Lord, you know because most people we were around, they didn't know much themselves. Nobody taught us about family life. And we've really been blessed that the Lord allowed us to learn through Him. You can't get no better teacher because most people [are] in turmoil in their own families including the preachers…

73. That's right. So with the children and all that, that had an impact on your life?

Then again, I say it was the Lord because I tell you the truth, Danny, as much as I can understand these children coming so fast, God gave me the love for children. I love children. I love my children. I can only give God the credit for that—that He allowed me to love my children. I don't think that I was ever abusive. I know that I might have been frustrated at times because when things don't come as easy as they could have come, you're gonna get frustrated—even as a Christian, even in Christ. But that's when the devil sneaks one on you. You know who is the source of your supply in life. But still sometimes that frustration could come in.

74. I can say as one of your children I know you weren't abusive.

But I didn't know a lot. I didn't.

75. Dad, I wish you had whipped me more. During

76

the first seven years of marriage with us coming along, was it tough as far as finances? I think we moved from Clifton Place to Tompkins and then to Johnson.

And from there to St. Marks. We moved in an apartment from Mother's. Oh, yes, I did. I moved from Clifton Place after we got married. And then you were born at Clifton Place. And we moved in with Mother and we moved out from Mother downtown back to...I may be mixed up there. But it seems then Mother bought a house. And I moved from downtown to Mother's on Johnson Street. A lot of moving.

76. So you moved to New York in '59?

I moved to Brooklyn, New York, in 1957. I worked on and off there.

77. And then you met Mom in '59 and got married in '60?

Yes.

78. And then all the children were born in New York?

All the children were born between '60 and '65. Every child was born within five years.

79. When did we leave Brooklyn?

We brought you all down like one year. We was able to go back to New York and live a little while because Aunt Betty came down and she stayed with you all here in Apalachicola, Florida, because she was either down here already and she kept you all down here. Mommy and I was able to go back to Brooklyn for a while to see how we could probably make it. It seems like you all were down here.

80. Because I remember coming down here and going to school and all that.

Yes. You all were down here for a while.

81. And you went back?

We went back. And then in 1968, this was after Dr. King got assassinated; by this time there was turmoil and chaos. After losing my brother, James, and then Dr. King, having lost President Kennedy—all these things were going on. Really now, I didn't think I was going to make it longer myself. And we come out of Brooklyn, New York, in 1968, moved to North Carolina, to make a life there. We moved there in 1968 and worked in Raleigh 'till '70. In July 1970 we had our house. Either we came to get you all or somebody brought you all.

82. So how long were we down in Florida before you came and got us?

Maybe a year or so. At least a year. Not less than a year because we went back. True enough. Then we started to come out of there. Because, see, one of the reasons why we brought you all home (I don't know what the plan was), but we didn't want to raise you all up in Brooklyn, New York. That was one thing Mommy said we didn't want to raise you all up in the state of New York 'cause we didn't want to move nowhere else in Brooklyn, New York or in Manhattan. We just didn't want you all to grow up there.

83. Okay, so it was Clifton Place?

Clifton Place

84. I'm not talking about the family. When you first got married it was Clifton Place. The second place was?

We moved to Mother's—Tompkins Avenue.

85. Then from Tompkins to?

I went to Evergreen Avenue.

86. Was that an apartment?

That was an apartment over at the Rev. Preacher's house.

87. And then after that it was Johnson Street?

No. After that it was downtown St. Marks. We moved into a larger apartment downtown St. Marks. We didn't stay there too long before Mother got her house...the Lord

79

blessed her. She got a new house. And then she wanted us to come live with her because she had this apartment which was still good. Some foolish times then, but it was still good because she was trying to help us.

88. During those first seven, eight, nine years with the kids coming like that, even though there were many good times, were there times frustrating and difficult as far as the financial part?

Yeah, it was. It was sometimes frustrating because I wasn't used to that magnitude of responsibility, and I believe that that would happen to anybody. But you know, going back to our Jewish people being so good to us, they helped us to make it in those crucial times. Because see, I worked for Jews most of the time while I was in New York City, in the fur market. I stayed with those jobs longer than I did with any other. So that's what helped us kind of make it. The people were good to us and we were able to make it.

89. Now where in there did you get into the relationship with the Lord and your life was changed?

Now, I told you it was about in 1961 when I first had this incredible experience. I didn't understand it. About the singing and how I jumped on my knees. I got out of bed, dropped on my knees, and told the Lord that whatever He wanted me to do that I would do, and what not. I was just inspired to do that at that time. Like I said, I did not follow through like I said I would. But it was there. After having made that statement without any understanding why, I was not really progressing. I was merely existing and what not. And I just know that even before I came to North Carolina, I made mention to Bro. Willis that I felt that the Lord had something even greater for me to do and instead of him criticizing me, he encouraged me.

That ends the interview that I did with my dad, Daniel White, Jr., sometime before he went home to be with the Lord. Indeed, from this point, my dad went on to be a loving father to his children and to do a great work for the glory of God in ministering to and loving other people. In his words, "love is what it is."

The Command to Honor Your Father

CHAPTER 6

Honour thy father and thy mother: that thy days may be long upon the land which the LORD thy God giveth thee.
(Exodus 20:12)

Children, obey your parents in the Lord: for this is right. Honour thy father and mother; which is the first commandment with promise; That it may be well with thee, and thou mayest live long on the earth.
(Ephesians 6:1-3)

Children, obey your parents in all things: for this is well pleasing unto the Lord.
(Colossians 3:20)

For God commanded, saying, Honour thy father and mother: and, He that curseth father or mother,

let him die the death.
(Matthew 15:4)

Hear, ye children, the instruction of a father, and attend
to know understanding. For I give you good doctrine,
forsake ye not my law. For I was my father's son, tender
and only beloved in the sight of my mother. He taught
me also, and said unto me, Let thine heart retain my
words: keep my commandments, and live.
(Proverbs 4 :1-4)

Hearken unto thy father that begat thee, and despise
not thy mother when she is old.
(Proverbs 23:22)

My son, hear the instruction of thy father,
and forsake not the law of thy mother: For they shall
be an ornament of grace unto thy head,
and chains about thy neck.
(Proverbs 1:8-9)

And, ye fathers, provoke not your children to wrath:
but bring them up in the nurture and admonition of
the Lord.
(Ephesians 6:4)

Fathers, provoke not your children to anger,
lest they be discouraged.
(Colossians 3:21)

Only take heed to thyself, and keep thy soul diligently,
lest thou forget the things which thine eyes have seen,
and lest they depart from thy heart all the days of thy
life: but teach them thy sons, and thy sons' sons.
(Deuteronomy 4:9)

Chasten thy son while there is hope, and let not
thy soul spare for his crying.
(Proverbs 19:18)

Train up a child in the way he should go: and when he is
old, he will not depart from it.
(Proverbs 22:6)

Withhold not correction from the child: for if thou
beatest him with the rod, he shall not die.
Thou shalt beat him with the rod, and shalt deliver
his soul from hell.
(Proverbs 23:13-14)

Correct thy son, and he shall give thee rest; yea, he shall
give delight unto thy soul.
(Proverbs 29:17)

What Great Men Have Said About Their Fathers

CHAPTER 7

Martin Luther King Jr.
"The thing that I admire most about my dad is his genuine Christian character. He is a man of real integrity, deeply committed to moral and ethical principles. He is conscientious in all of his undertakings. Even the person who disagrees with his frankness has to admit that his motives and actions are sincere."

Michael Jordan
"When I think of my career, where I have come from, where it all began, and all that I have accomplished along the way, I realize everything did change after that game. Not just basketball, but my life. I think my father saw some things in me that I couldn't see in myself. At first, I just thought it was a father's pride, the voice of hopes and dreams for a son to be successful. I saw his comments more in the

context of a motivational speech a father might give a son. I do believe my father knew. I believe he saw things unfolding in a way that no one, not me, not the Chicago Bulls, or anyone else saw. I believe that's a father's gift."

Ryan Dobson
"I see intolerance in my dad who takes a stand on a daily basis no matter what anybody says. He does what God wants him to do, even though people don't like it—a lot of people. They put him down and take him off the air because he makes a stand for Christ. And he does it anyway. He could take the easy way out. When he was on the gambling and pornography commission, we got threats from the Mafia. He could have said, 'You know what? Enough of this,' but he did what God wanted him to do."

Colin Powell
When I was a boy growing up in the South Bronx, my father was the dominant figure in my life. A Jamaican immigrant like my mother, who worked his way up to a foreman's job in Manhattan's garment district, Luther Powell never let his race or station affect his sense of self. West Indians like him had come to this country with nothing. Every morning they got on the subway, worked like dogs all day, got home at 8 at night, supported their families and educated their children. If they could do that, how dare anyone think they were less than anybody's equal? That was Pop's attitude, and it became mine, too. At home, my father was the neighborhood Solomon--the village wiseman people came to for advice, for domestic arbitration or for help in getting a job. He would bring

home clothes, seconds and irregulars, and end bolts of fabric from the company where he worked, and sell them at wholesale or give them to anybody in need. He was totally unimpressed by rank, place, or ceremony. Once, when I was a colonel stationed at Fort Campbell, Kentucky, I invited my parents to join us for Thanksgiving dinner. My father talked with generals as if he had known generals all his life, and then table hopped through the mess hall, like Omar Bradley mixing with the troops before an invasion. I was struck by his total aplomb: Luther Powell belonged wherever Luther Powell happened to be. He was a short man, just 5 feet 2 inches tall; but, like Napoleon, he was masterful.

Tiger Woods
My dad has always taught me these words: care and share. That's why we put on clinics. The only thing I can do is try to give back.

George Foreman IV
My dad is a great mentor and a great father. Even now that we're so far apart, we stay up-to-date on each other's lives every day. We have a great relationship. He's always there for me.

Anthony Evans
My dad made me understand that living for the Lord was real. It wasn't because of the church, programs, books or radio it was simply because of the way he lived. As a child of a minister I was more focused on his life at home being congruent with his life at the church...it was and now I

stand confident in what I do...My dad made sure that we got away for family vacations and that he was able to take me horseback riding and to basketball games. He is very focused on family.

John Marshall
My father, Thurgood Marshall, was a man who loved his family, his God and his country.

Jeremy White
My father, Reggie White was an honest, humble, honorable, dedicated, determined, passionate, and caring man...He was a compassionate father, a loving husband, a selfless friend, and a loyal teammate. I know that he will be an inspiration to countless people who want to make their dream a reality, whatever their dream might be.

Tim Russert
The older I get, the smarter my father seems to get. I have learned so much from Big Russ, and I feel so grateful to him, that I wanted to write a book about the two of us...Whatever we achieve and whoever we are, we stand on our father's shoulders.

Jim Valvano
My father gave me the greatest gift anyone could give another person, he believed in me.

President Barack Obama
Talks About the Importance of Black Men Staying with Their Children and Being Great Fathers

CHAPTER 8

At the end of the Sermon on the Mount, Jesus closes by saying, *"Whoever hears these words of mine, and does them, shall be likened to a wise man who built his house upon a rock: and the rain descended, and the floods came, and the winds blew, and beat upon that house, and it fell not, for it was founded upon a rock"* (Matthew 7: 24-25).

Here at Apostolic, you are blessed to worship in a house that has been founded on the rock of Jesus Christ, our Lord and Savior. But it is also built on another rock, another foundation—and that rock is Bishop Arthur Brazier. In forty-eight years, he has built this congregation from just a few hundred to more than 20,000 strong—a congregation that, because of his leadership, has braved the fierce winds and heavy rains of violence and poverty; joblessness and hopelessness. Because of his work and his ministry, there are more graduates and fewer gang members in the neighborhoods surrounding this church. There are more homes and fewer homeless. There is more community and less chaos because Bishop Brazier continued the march for justice that he began by Dr. King's side all those years ago. He is the reason this house has stood tall for half a century. And on this Father's Day, it must make him proud to know that the man now charged with keeping its foundation strong is his son and your new pastor, Reverend Byron Brazier.

Of all the rocks upon which we build our lives, we are reminded today that family is the most important. And we are called to recognize and honor how critical every father is to that foundation. They are teachers and coaches. They are mentors and role models. They are examples of success and the men who constantly push us toward it.

But if we are honest with ourselves, we'll admit that what too many fathers also are is missing—missing from too many lives and too many homes. They have abandoned their responsibilities, acting like boys instead of men. And the foundations of our families are weaker because of it.

You and I know how true this is in the African-American community. We know that more than half of all black children live in single-parent households, a number that has doubled—doubled—since we were children. We know the statistics—that children who grow up without a father are five times more likely to live in poverty and commit crime; nine times more likely to drop out of schools and twenty times more likely to end up in prison. They are more likely to have behavioral problems, or run away from home, or become teenage parents themselves. And the foundations of our community are weaker because of it.

How many times in the last year has this city lost a child at the hands of another child? How many times have our hearts stopped in the middle of the night with the sound of a gunshot or a siren? How many teenagers have we seen hanging around on street corners when they should be sitting in a classroom? How many are sitting in prison when they should be working, or at least looking for a job? How many in this generation are we willing to lose to poverty or violence or addiction? How many?

Yes, we need more cops on the street. Yes, we need fewer guns in the hands of people who shouldn't have them. Yes, we need more money for our schools, and more outstanding teachers in the classroom, and more afterschool programs for our children. Yes, we need more jobs and more job training and more opportunity in our communities.

But we also need families to raise our children. We need fathers to realize that responsibility does not end at conception. We need them to realize that what makes you a man is not the ability to have a child—it's the courage to raise one.

We need to help all the mothers out there who are raising

these kids by themselves; the mothers who drop them off at school, go to work, pick them up in the afternoon, work another shift, get dinner, make lunches, pay the bills, fix the house, and all the other things it takes both parents to do. So many of these women are doing a heroic job, but they need support. They need another parent. Their children need another parent. That's what keeps their foundation strong. It's what keeps the foundation of our country strong.

I know what it means to have an absent father, although my circumstances weren't as tough as they are for many young people today. Even though my father left us when I was two years old, and I only knew him from the letters he wrote and the stories that my family told, I was luckier than most. I grew up in Hawaii, and had two wonderful grandparents from Kansas who poured everything they had into helping my mother raise my sister and me—who worked with her to teach us about love and respect and the obligations we have to one another. I screwed up more often than I should've, but I got plenty of second chances. And even though we didn't have a lot of money, scholarships gave me the opportunity to go to some of the best schools in the country. A lot of kids don't get these chances today. There is no margin for error in their lives. So my own story is different in that way.

Still, I know the toll that being a single parent took on my mother—how she struggled at times to the pay bills; to give us the things that other kids had; to play all the roles that both parents are supposed to play. And I know the

94

toll it took on me. So I resolved many years ago that it was my obligation to break the cycle—that if I could be anything in life, I would be a good father to my girls; that if I could give them anything, I would give them that rock—that foundation—on which to build their lives. And that would be the greatest gift I could offer.

I say this knowing that I have been an imperfect father—knowing that I have made mistakes and will continue to make more; wishing that I could be home for my girls and my wife more than I am right now. I say this knowing all of these things because even as we are imperfect, even as we face difficult circumstances, there are still certain lessons we must strive to live and learn as fathers—whether we are black or white; rich or poor; from the South Side or the wealthiest suburb.

The first is setting an example of excellence for our children—because if we want to set high expectations for them, we've got to set high expectations for ourselves. It's great if you have a job; it's even better if you have a college degree. It's a wonderful thing if you are married and living in a home with your children, but don't just sit in the house and watch "SportsCenter" all weekend long. That's why so many children are growing up in front of the television. As fathers and parents, we've got to spend more time with them, and help them with their homework, and replace the video game or the remote control with a book once in awhile. That's how we build that foundation.

We know that education is everything to our children's

95

future. We know that they will no longer just compete for good jobs with children from Indiana, but children from India and China and all over the world. We know the work and the studying and the level of education that requires.

You know, sometimes I'll go to an eighth-grade graduation and there's all that pomp and circumstance and gowns and flowers. And I think to myself, it's just eighth grade. To really compete, they need to graduate high school, and then they need to graduate college, and they probably need a graduate degree too. An eighth-grade education doesn't cut it today. Let's give them a handshake and tell them to get their butts back in the library!

It's up to us—as fathers and parents—to instill this ethic of excellence in our children. It's up to us to say to our daughters, don't ever let images on TV tell you what you are worth, because I expect you to dream without limit and reach for those goals. It's up to us to tell our sons, those songs on the radio may glorify violence, but in my house we live glory to achievement, self respect, and hard work. It's up to us to set these high expectations. And that means meeting those expectations ourselves. That means setting examples of excellence in our own lives.

The second thing we need to do as fathers is pass along the value of empathy to our children. Not sympathy, but empathy—the ability to stand in somebody else's shoes; to look at the world through their eyes. Sometimes it's so easy to get caught up in "us," that we forget about our obligations to one another. There's a culture in our society that says remembering these obligations is somehow soft—that we can't show weakness, and so therefore we can't show kindness.

But our young boys and girls see that. They see when you are ignoring or mistreating your wife. They see when you are inconsiderate at home; or when you are distant; or when you are thinking only of yourself. And so it's no surprise when we see that behavior in our schools or on our streets. That's why we pass on the values of empathy and kindness to our children by living them. We need to show our kids that you're not strong by putting other people down—you're strong by lifting them up. That's our responsibility as fathers.

And by the way—it's a responsibility that also extends to Washington. Because if fathers are doing their part; if they're taking their responsibilities seriously to be there for their children, and set high expectations for them, and instill in them a sense of excellence and empathy, then our government should meet them halfway.

We should be making it easier for fathers who make responsible choices and harder for those who avoid them. We should get rid of the financial penalties we impose on married couples right now, and start making sure that every dime of child support goes directly to helping children instead of some bureaucrat. We should reward fathers who pay that child support with job training and job opportunities and a larger Earned Income Tax Credit that can help them pay the bills. We should expand programs where registered nurses visit expectant and new mothers and help them learn how to care for themselves before the baby is born and what to do after—programs that have helped increase father involvement, women's employment, and children's readiness for school. We should help these new families care for their children by expanding maternity and paternity leave, and we should guarantee every worker more paid sick leave so they can stay home to take care of their child without losing their income.

We should take all of these steps to build a strong foundation for our children. But we should also know that even if we do; even if we meet our obligations as fathers and parents; even if Washington does its part too, we will still face difficult challenges in our lives. There will still be days of struggle and heartache. The rains will still come and the winds will still blow.

And that is why the final lesson we must learn as fathers is also the greatest gift we can pass on to our children—and that is the gift of hope.

I'm not talking about an idle hope that's little more than blind optimism or willful ignorance of the problems we face. I'm talking about hope as that spirit inside us that insists, despite all evidence to the contrary, that something better is waiting for us if we're willing to work for it and fight for it. If we are willing to believe.

I was answering questions at a town hall meeting in

Wisconsin the other day and a young man raised his hand, and I figured he'd ask about college tuition or energy or maybe the war in Iraq. But instead he looked at me very seriously and he asked, "What does life mean to you?"

Now, I have to admit that I wasn't quite prepared for that one. I think I stammered for a little bit, but then I stopped and gave it some thought, and I said this:

When I was a young man, I thought life was all about me—how do I make my way in the world, and how do I become successful and how do I get the things that I want.

But now, my life revolves around my two little girls. And what I think about is what kind of world I'm leaving them. Are they living in a country where there's a huge gap between a few who are wealthy and a whole bunch of people who are struggling every day? Are they living in a country that is still divided by race? A country where, because they're girls, they don't have as much opportunity as boys do? Are they living in a country where we are hated around the world because we don't cooperate effectively with other nations? Are they living in a world that is in grave danger because of what we've done to its climate?

And what I've realized is that life doesn't count for much unless you're willing to do your small part to leave our children—all of our children—a better world. Even if it's difficult. Even if the work seems great. Even if we don't get very far in our lifetime.

That is our ultimate responsibility as fathers and parents. We try. We hope. We do what we can to build our house upon the sturdiest rock. And when the winds come, and the rains fall, and they beat upon that house, we keep faith that our Father will be there to guide us, and watch over us, and protect us, and lead His children through the darkest of storms into light of a better day. That is my prayer for all of us on this Father's Day, and that is my hope for this country in the years ahead. May God Bless you and your children. Thank you.

Fatherhood
by George Foreman

CHAPTER 9

In his book, *Fatherhood by George*, the boxing champion gloves up for parenting. Sharing from his childhood and fatherhood experiences, the parent of 10 offers his personal stories, insights and advice on how to be a winning dad. Here is an excerpt:

Run for your life
Drifting out in space, isolated, far away from the gravitational pull of the earth—just hanging around without direction, nothing to keep me grounded—no course to run on, no path to follow. That's what it felt like for me growing up fatherless. What I lacked and desperately needed was the strong arm of guidance, that stabilizing, grounding force that only a loving father can give.

My mama tried her best to fulfill the roles of both mother

and father. She was wonderful and tender, giving me all of her gentle love and care. Because I was so big, Mama always saw to it that I had a little extra food. She'd even let me eat off her plate. Like most good mothers, she sacrificed much for me and would do just about anything for her boy. Yet there was one thing Mama couldn't do no matter how hard she tried: she couldn't be a father. Oh, how she longed to be that strong arm of guidance that I needed, but as I grew older and more adamant, she would often fall short. Eventually, my rebellious and stubborn nature, coupled with my intimidating size, simply wore her down. In the end, all she could do was turn me over to the Lord. I can remember that day so vividly. Mama, frustrated and tired, looked up at her teenage giant and said, "Son, I just can't do it anymore. You're too much to handle. I'm turning you over to the Lord."

Now, that may not sound very threatening to some, but make no mistake about it, turning me over to the Lord was not a passive move on her part. It was something my mama took very seriously. She knew she couldn't manhandle me or protect me from the pressures and temptations of the world anymore. So, through the tears and pain that only a loving mother can know, she committed herself to prayer, leaving me to the Lord for Him to do whatever He needed in order to get my attention. And I'm here to tell you that the Lord answered her prayers.

In the scripture at the beginning of this chapter, Solomon, the author, plainly shows it is the father's job to guide his children and that children are smart when they pay attention to fatherly advice. And although Solomon's writing was directed to the children of God universally, as he continued to develop his thoughts in this passage he wrote about the impact his own father, David, had in his life: *"My children, listen when your father corrects you. Pay attention and learn good judgment, for I am giving you good guidance. Don't turn away from my instructions. For I too, was once my father's son, tenderly loved as my mother's only child. My father taught me, 'Take my words to heart. Follow my commands, and you will live'"* (Proverbs 4:1–4). What did David mean when he told his son Solomon, *"Take my words to heart. Follow my commands and you will live"*? In essence, he meant that it was his responsibility as a father to lead and direct his son in the ways of life, to a place where he could reach his full potential as a person, and by heeding his father's advice, Solomon could avoid the pitfalls that lead to destruction.

The call of fatherhood is to be a strong arm of guidance— a consistent blend of love, strength, respect, friendship, teaching, and discipline. But when the father-presence is absent and the mother is unable to fulfill the role, God often has to use other methods as the strong arm of direction. Many times those other methods are brutal. For me, those methods began with a run-in with the law.

After Mama had turned me over to the Lord, it didn't take very long for the Lord to start working. On one particular night the police were looking for me because I'd been involved in an illegal activity. To say I was scared would have been an understatement. I was terrified—more than I had been in my entire life. So, as a reaction to my fear, I instinctively started to run. The whole time I was running, a voice kept thundering in my mind and I knew it was the voice of God. He told me, "Okay, George, you want to run from rules? You want to run from authority and from what your mother says? Well, George, let's run now. Let's run for your life."

Up to that point, I had seen myself as invincible, that nothing could really happen to me. Yet there I was, running for my life, from the police, trying to find a place to hide. They were chasing me like I was a common criminal, and I knew if I got caught that I was going straight to jail. They even had dogs with them to sniff me out. While trying to hide, a scene from a movie replayed in my mind. Some escaped prisoners were running from tracking dogs, and they jumped into a creek to break their scent. With this scene playing in my mind, I crawled into a busted sewer pipe and laid there, hoping the dogs wouldn't smell me. Hiding there in that foul, stinky, nasty pipe, hearing the cops' voices getting closer and closer, thinking about those dogs coming at me, tearing me apart and then going to jail, for the first time it dawned on me that I was no different from those men in the movie. I had done wrong and I was a criminal. All the things Mama had told me started coming to my mind, especially, "George, I'm turning you over to the Lord." It was then that I said to myself, "If I get out of this sewer pipe, I will never break the law again. I'm going to make something of my life!" Looking back, that was the beginning of my transformation, but it took many years and the Lord using many more of life's hard methods for me to learn what I needed to learn. Years later, when I became a father myself, I determined I was going to be that strong arm of guidance and stabilizing, grounding force that my children would need in their lives.

The impact of fatherlessness in our world today is far reaching—from high-paid athletes doing foolish things, to inmates in maximum security prisons, to children making poor life choices. Consider for a moment the raw statistics. Roughly 85 percent of youth in prison today come from fatherless homes. Ninety percent of homeless kids or runaways are fatherless. Sixty-three percent of youth suicides were fatherless, as are 71 percent of high school dropouts.

Often when I go into prisons to minister or I'm counseling a professional athlete, it becomes obvious to me that many of them are craving a father figure. They may be big and physical on the outside, but inside there's a little boy asleep who doesn't know what to do. They're reaping the effects of poor choices, and I believe a significant reason they've made these poor choices is because of the absence of a father figure in their lives. Every child growing up desperately needs a David or Solomon who will say to them and model before them, *"Take my words to heart. Follow my commands, and you will live."* And that is what this book is all about. Whether you're a brand new father, a father of a teenager, or even a seasoned veteran of an adult child, it's about you seizing the moment and becoming the father-presence God intended you to be. Think about it. If fatherlessness has the power to affect our world in such a negative way, then imagine the influence a loving father has to shape his children and thus the world in a positive way. Ken Canfield couldn't have said it better when he wrote in his book, *The Heart of a Father*, "A father has enormous power. About this, he has no choice. For good or for bad, by his presence or absence, action or inaction, whether abusive or nurturing, the fact remains: A father is one of the most powerful beings on the face of the earth."

Excerpted from "Fatherhood by George: Hard-Won Advice on Being a Dad" by George Foreman.

The Importance of Fathers Staying

CHAPTER 10

I cannot stress enough that the greatest thing my father ever did for me was staying with our family. That is why I am writing this book—to honor my father. I know that I am stronger and better because of my father's sacrifice. However, even though there are many other fathers who choose to stay with their families and raise their children, there are even more fathers who choose not to do what my father did. Statistics show that children who do not grow up with fathers in the home are worse off than the children who do.

According to Rebecca O'Neill of CIVITAS, "the experiment has failed:"

For the best part of thirty years we have been conducting a vast experiment with the family, and now the results are in: the decline of the two-parent, married-couple family has resulted in poverty, ill-health, educational failure, unhappiness, anti-social behaviour, isolation and social exclusion for thousands of women, men and children. *(Source: Experiments in Living: The Fatherless Family, September 2002)*

Here are statistics on children without fathers in the home:

- 63% of youth suicides are from fatherless homes *(US Dept. Of Health/Census)* – 5 times the average.

- 90% of all homeless and runaway children are from fatherless homes – 32 times the average.

- 85% of all children who show behavior disorders come from fatherless homes – 20 times the average. *(Center for Disease Control)*

- 80% of rapists with anger problems come from fatherless homes – 14 times the average. *(Justice & Behavior, Vol 14, p. 403-26)*

- 71% of all high school dropouts come from fatherless homes – 9 times the average. *(National Principals Association Report)*

- 75% of all adolescent patients in chemical abuse centers come from fatherless homes – 10 times the average. *(Rainbows for All God's Children)*

- 70% of youths in state-operated institutions come from fatherless homes – 9 times the average. *(U.S. Dept. of Justice, Sept. 1988)*

- 85% of all youths in prison come from fatherless homes – 20 times the average. *(Fulton Co. Georgia, Texas Dept. of Correction)*

Also, notice the following:

Children in father-absent homes are five times more likely to be poor. In 2002, 7.8 percent of children in married-couple families were living in poverty, compared to 38.4 percent of children in female-householder families. *(U.S. Census Bureau, 2003)*

Compared to living with both parents, living in a single-parent home doubles the risk that a child will suffer physical, emotional, or educational neglect. The overall rate of child abuse and neglect in single-parent households is 27.3 children per 1,000, whereas the rate of overall maltreatment in two-parent households is 15.5 per 1,000. *(America's Children, 1997)*

If you are still not convinced, you can find many more statistics by going online and searching for "fatherless children" and "statistics on fatherless children." It is clear that a father being in the life of a child is very important. Yes, mothers play an important role, but they cannot raise children by themselves. A child needs both parents in the home. Being a father is a very special role and opportunity. Fathers, may I encourage you to take it seriously and be the best father to your child that you can be. It is important for fathers to stay.

Great Black Fathers Besides My Own Father

CHAPTER 11

TONY DUNGY

Tony Dungy (born October 6, 1955) is a former professional football player and coach in the National Football League. Dungy was head coach of the Tampa Bay Buccaneers from 1996 to 2001, and head coach of the Indianapolis Colts from 2002 to 2008. He became the first black head coach to win the Super Bowl on February 4, 2007. Dungy is a devout evangelical Christian and at one point in his coaching career considered leaving football for the prison ministry. He began a mentoring program for young people called Mentors for Life. Throughout his career, he has remained involved with community service organizations. He is married to Lauren Harris of Pittsburgh and has two daughters, Tiara and Jade, and four sons, Eric, Jordan, Justin, and James Dungy (deceased).

REV. MARTIN LUTHER KING, SR.

Reverend Martin Luther King, Sr. (December 19, 1899 – November 11, 1984), was a Baptist minister, an advocate for social justice, an early civil rights leader and the father of Martin Luther King, Jr. King, Sr. led the Ebenezer Baptist Church in Atlanta, Georgia, and became a leader of the civil rights movement, as the head of the NAACP chapter in Atlanta and of the Civic and Political League. Daddy King encouraged his son to become active in the civil rights movement and was the inspiration behind his son's ministry.

DR. BEN CARSON

Dr. Ben Carson is a world famous neurosurgeon who became the director of pediatric neurosurgery at Johns Hopkins Hospital when he was just 33 years old. Carson married Candy Rustin—whom he met at Yale—in 1975. Both are devout evangelical Christians and members of the Seventh-day Adventist Church. They have three sons, Murray, Benjamin Jr., and Rhoeyce. He and their sons comprise the Carson Four, an accomplished string quartet. Early in his career, Carson and his wife developed the idea for the Carson Scholars Fund, to provide scholarships for promising young people who lack the money for school. The group recognizes young people of all backgrounds for exceptional academic and humanitarian accomplishments.

DR. TONY EVANS

Dr. Evans serves as Senior Pastor to the over 7,500 member Oak Cliff Bible Fellowship in Dallas, Texas. He is also founder and president of The Urban Alternative. He was the first black American to earn a doctorate in Theology from Dallas Theological Seminary. Dr. Evans is married to Lois, his wife and co-laborer in ministry. He is the father of four: Chrystal, Priscilla, Anthony, Jr., and Jonathan. He and Lois are the proud grandparents of six children: Kariss, Jessica, Jackson, Tre, J.C. and Kanaan. Chrystal leads and ministers with the praise and worship team at Oak Cliff Bible Fellowship. Priscilla Shirer is married to Jerry Shirer, and she runs Going Beyond Ministries. Anthony Evans, is a Christian singer with three studio albums (Letting Go, Even More, and The Bridge). Jonathan Evans, is a professional football player in the National Football League.

REV. JOHN WESLEY RICE, JR.

The Rev. John Wesley Rice, Jr. rose from the segregated South to become a minister and university leader. Dr. Rice was born in Baton Rouge, Louisiana. He worked as a Presbyterian minister, teacher and coach at a high school in Birmingham, Alabama before becoming dean of students at Stillman College in Tuscaloosa. In 1969, he became a professor and assistant vice chancellor of the University of Denver. He is the father of Condoleezza Rice, who was selected by former President George W. Bush to be his national security adviser, and went on to serve as secretary of state.

REV. KEVIN D. BARNES, SR.

The Reverend Kevin D. Barnes, Sr. was born and raised in Donaldsonville, Louisiana. He comes from a family that loves the Lord, and taught him the way of the Lord. He is married to the lovely Brenda Barnes and is the father of three sons, Kevin Jr., Keith, and Kenneth Barnes, who serve in the music ministry of Abyssinian Missionary Baptist Church, where Barnes is the pastor. Dr. Barnes received his Ph.D. in May 2007 from Sacramento Theological Seminary Bible College. He is also the author of the Amazon.com Bestseller, *Successfully Raising Young Black Men.*

EARL WOODS

Earl Dennison Woods (March 5, 1932 – May 3, 2006) was an athlete, a US Army infantry officer, (retiring as a Lieutenant Colonel), and the father of golfer, Tiger Woods. Woods was born in Manhattan, Kansas, where he was raised by Maude Carter and Miles Woods. He was the youngest and the only male of four siblings. His second marriage produced his fourth child, Eldrick, who was given the nickname "Tiger." Tiger became a child prodigy in golf by the time he was three years old. Earl Woods shared many of the techniques he used in rearing Tiger in two books: *Training a Tiger* and *Playing Through: Straight Talk on Hard Work, Big Dreams and Adventures with Tiger.*

PASTOR TOMMY STEELE

Pastor Steele is the senior pastor of New Life Independent Baptist Church, in Concord, North Carolina. He is the recipient of many honors including an honorary Doctorate of Theology Degree. He is married to Tonda Bostick Steele. They have two sons, Gary and Joshua. Gary Steele serves as the assistant pastor at New Life; Joshua Steele is the church's music minister.

FRASER ROBINSON III

Fraser Robinson lll was not really famous in life. But he was First Lady Michelle Obama's dad. He was able to live, work, provide for his family, and raise his children even though he had multiple sclerosis. Fraser was born on August 1, 1935 in Chicago. He was a pump worker for the City of Chicago. He tended the boilers at a water-filtration plant. Mr. Robinson developed multiple sclerosis as a young man. In spite of having this disease, he continued working and, according to Michelle Obama, he hardly ever missed a day of work. Michelle told how she would see her father walk to work using two canes. Even though he had to sometimes struggle to get ready for work, he knew this was what he needed to do. He was also active on the political front. Fraser Robinson was a Democratic Precinct Captain. He and his wife, Marianne, valued hard work, independence, and honesty and they worked together to instill these values in their children.

REV. DWIGHT MCKISSICK

Rev. Dwight McKissic is one of the most prominent African-American Southern Baptist ministers and is the senior pastor of Cornerstone Baptist Church in Arlington, Texas and is the founder of Cornerstone Academy. He is married to Vera McKissic. All of their children serve with them in the ministry.

DR. LOU BALDWIN

God called Lou Baldwin to the Gospel ministry shortly after his conversion in 1976. He along with his wife, Jeanette, and three children were soon commissioned to plant what is now the thriving Crossroads Baptist Church in Bailey's Crossroads, Virginia. As the senior pastor, he is known for his powerful, practical preaching, and his consistent stand on Biblical principles and standards. He is a visionary with a compassion for people and a great love for children. His teaching and counsel have helped hundreds of families and individuals become the best that they can be for God. He and his wife, Jeanette, have two sons, Michael and Kenny, who serve on Dr. Baldwin's ministerial staff. His daughter, Dee Dee, is a teacher in the church's Christian Academy. His son-in-law (Lou), two daughters-in-law (Lora and Bethany) and nine grandchildren are all very active in the ministry as well.

RICHARD WILLIAMS

Richard Williams (born 1942) is an American tennis coach. He is best known for being the father of Serena and Venus Williams, both former World No.1 tennis players and multi-grand slam winners. Wanting a better future for his five daughters, and wanting at least one of them to succeed in sports, Richard Williams began to take them to the Compton public tennis courts, soon after getting them into California tennis tournaments. His daughter Serena won the US Open in 1999, before her eighteenth birthday.

BILL COSBY

Bill Cosby (born July 12, 1937) is a philanthropist, comedian, actor, author, television producer, musician and activist. During the 1980s, Cosby produced and starred in what is considered one of the decade's defining sitcoms, "The Cosby Show," which lasted eight seasons from 1984 to 1992, and is still seen in syndication. The sitcom highlighted the experiences and growth of an upper middle-class African-American family. He also produced the hit sitcom, "A Different World," which became second to "The Cosby Show" in ratings. His good-natured, fatherly image and advice has made him a popular personality and garnered him the nickname of "America's Dad."

BUCK FRANKLIN

Buck Colbert Franklin (1879-1960) is the father of the famous, John Hope Franklin. He led an extraordinary life; from his boyhood adventures on a ranch in what was then the Indian Territory to his practice of law in twentieth-century Tulsa, he was an observant witness to the changes in politics, law, daily existence, and race relations that transformed the wide-open Southwest. After returning from college in the foreign worlds of Nashville and Atlanta, Franklin married a college classmate, studied law by mail, passed the bar, and struggled to build a practice in Ardmore and, later, in the all-black town of Rentiesville during the first years of Oklahoma's statehood. Buck Franklin, said of his children, "We have three children of whom I am very proud. Mozella Franklin-Jones, Buck Colbert Franklin, Jr., and John Hope Franklin."

GEN. COLIN POWELL

General Colin Powell was the chairman of the Joint Chiefs of Staff under Presidents Bush and Clinton and the highest-ranking member of the U.S. Armed Forces. Powell married Alma Johnson on August 25, 1962. Their son, Michael, is the former chairman of the Federal Communications Commission. In March 2006, Michael became a Trustee of the RAND Corporation. On April 21, 2006, Michael was elected the Rector of the Board of Visitors at the College of William and Mary, making him the first African-American to serve in that post in the College's 313 year history.

JOSEPH JACKSON

SPECIAL NOTE: We are well aware of the controversy surrounding the Jackson family. however, we took the liberty to place Joe Jackson in this list because he is one of those rare fathers who exemplified the ability to discern the talents of his children and guided them in the path of their gifts to great success for their lives at an early age. Of course, we urge all Christian fathers to do the same, but for the glory of God.

Joseph Walter "Joe" Jackson (born July 26, 1929) is a manager, former boxer, former musician, best known as the father of American entertainers, Michael and Janet Jackson. He is also notable for forming The Jackson 5, a Motown group that became popular in the early 1970s. By 1964, Joe had discovered that his three eldest sons, Jackie, Tito and Jermaine, had musical talent. After Tito played for him with Jackie and Jermaine backing up vocally, he helped form an early incarnation of The Jackson 5 with two neighborhood youths though eventually younger brothers Marlon and Michael joined. Within a few years, the Jackson 5 polished their talents under Joseph's strict leadership. Jackson's contributions to his children's success led to him being honored by the Rock & Roll Hall of Fame as "the greatest musical manager of all time."

FREDERICK DOUGLASS
American abolitionist, editor, orator, author, statesman, and former slave provided a new model for African-Americans and taught his son, Lewis, to live as a free man...By taking his son, Lewis, with him to important meetings and standing up for him during struggles, he reinforced his strongest beliefs and set a shining example for all to live, not under bondage, but as free people.

JAMES JORDAN
James Raymond Jordan, Sr. (July 31, 1936 – July 23, 1993) was the father of the basketball superstar, Michael Jordan and Army Command Sergeant Major James R. Jordan, Jr. A life-long basketball fan, Jordan had played a large role in inspiring his son, Michael, to become an athlete. Jordan was a businessman and traveled the country to follow Michael's career, first at the University of North Carolina and then with the Chicago Bulls. He was killed in a robbery near Lumberton, North Carolina.

PRESIDENT BARACK OBAMA
Barack Obama is the 44th President of the United States. He is the first African American to hold the office. Obama was the junior United States Senator from Illinois from January 2005 until November 2008, when he resigned after his election to the presidency. He and First Lady Michelle

Obama were married in 1992. The couple's first daughter, Malia Ann, was born in 1998, followed by a second daughter, Natasha ("Sasha"), in 2001. In a letter to his daughters in *PARADE* magazine, Obama wrote: "These are the things I want for you—to grow up in a world with no limits on your dreams and no achievements beyond your reach, and to grow into compassionate, committed women who will help build that world. And I want every child to have the same chances to learn and dream and grow and thrive that you girls have..."

DENZEL WASHINGTON, JR.

Denzel Washington, Jr. (born December 28, 1954) is an American actor, screenwriter, director and film producer. He has garnered much critical acclaim for his work in film since the 1990s, including for his portrayals. Washington has been awarded three Golden Globe awards and two Academy Awards for his work. He is notable as the second African-American man (after Sidney Poitier) to win the Academy Award for Best Actor, which he received for his role in the 2001 film "Training Day." He is the father of four children, including 23-year-old John David, who signed a football contract with the St. Louis Rams in 2006; 20-year-old Katia, who is attending Yale University; and 17-year-old twins, Olivia and Malcolm.

HERBERT AARON

Herbert Aaron taught his son Henry "Hank" Aaron the importance of excellence, education, and patience. Henry would go on to hit 755 home runs over a 23-year career to become the major league's all-time home-run king. In the book *Chasing the Dream*, Henry commented that years of watching his father labor long and hard for his family taught him the value of patience and respect. These were traits that young Henry would emulate, especially later in his career as he faced persecution and racial hatred while nearing Babe Ruth's home-run record....Henry grew up in a close, nurturing family, where he was expected to behave, respect elders, cut firewood, and go to church on Sundays. Herbert and his wife, raised their children in a loving home with their greatest good in mind.

MATHEW KNOWLES

Mathew Knowles (born January 9, 1951) is a music executive and manager. He is the father and manager of singers, Beyoncé Knowles and sister, Solange, and is best known as the manager of the female R&B group, Destiny's Child. He is married to Tina Knowles. He founded and operates the Music World Entertainment record label imprint. He and his family are members of St. John's Methodist Church in Houston, Texas.

Powerful Words About the Importance of Fathers

CHAPTER 12

By profession, I am a soldier and take pride in that fact. But I am prouder, infinitely prouder, to be a father.

- General Douglas MacArthur

&

A truly rich man is one whose children run into his arms when his hands are empty.

- Author Unknown

&

Love and fear. Everything the father of a family says must inspire one or the other.

- Joseph Joubert

Henry James once defined life as that predicament which precedes death, and certainly nobody owes you a debt of honor or gratitude for getting him into that predicament. But a child does owe his father a debt, if Dad, having gotten him into this peck of trouble, takes off his coat and buckles down to the job of showing his son how best to crash through it.

- Clarence Budington Kelland

Sometimes the poorest man leaves his children the richest inheritance.

- Ruth E. Renkel

Nothing I've ever done has given me more joys and rewards than being a father to my children.

- Bill Cosby

A father carries pictures where his money used to be.

- Author Unknown

The father who would taste the essence of his fatherhood must turn back from the plane of his experience, take with him the fruits of his journey and begin again beside his child, marching step by step over the same old road.

- Angelo Patri

&

My father, when he went, made my childhood a gift of a half a century.

- Antonio Porchia

&

It is much easier to become a father than to be one.

- Kent Nerburn

&

The words that a father speaks to his children in the privacy of home are not heard by the world, but, as in whispering-galleries, they are clearly heard at the end and by posterity.

- Jean Paul Richter

&

Sherman made the terrible discovery that men make about their fathers sooner or later... that the man before him was not an aging father but a boy, a boy much like himself, a boy who grew up and had a child of his own and, as best he could, out of a sense of duty and, perhaps love, adopted a role called Being a Father so that his child would have something mythical and infinitely important:

a Protector, who would keep a lid on all the chaotic and catastrophic possibilities of life.

- Tom Wolfe

Fathers represent another way of looking at life—the possibility of an alternative dialogue.

- Louise J. Kaplan

There's something like a line of gold thread running through a man's words when he talks to his daughter, and gradually over the years it gets to be long enough for you to pick up in your hands and weave into a cloth that feels like love itself.

- John Gregory Brown

He was all questions. But small boys expect their fathers to be walking lexicons, to do two jobs at once, to give replies as they are working, whether laying stones or building models...digging up a shrub, or planting flower beds....Boys have a right to ask their fathers questions...Fathers are the powers that be, and with their power and might must shelter, guard, and hold and teach and love...All men with sons must learn to do these things...Too soon, too soon, a small son grows and leaves his father's side to test his manhood's wings. - Roy Z. Kemp

It's clear that most American children suffer too much mother and too little father.

- Gloria Steinem

Role modeling is the most basic responsibility of parents. Parents are handing life's scripts to their children, scripts that in all likelihood will be acted out for the rest of the children's lives.

- Stephen R. Covey

My father was not a failure. After all, he was the father of a president of the United States.

- Harry S. Truman

Directly after God in heaven comes a papa.

- W. A. Mozart

I know that I will never find my father in any other man who comes into my life, because it is a void in my life that can only be filled by him.

- Halle Berry

So we could all have heroes, God gave us dads.

- Glenda Allen

❧

Where would we be without fathers? Up to our necks in utility bills, getting bad mileage from out-of-balance tires, and in desperate need of an oil change.

- Linda Barnes

❧

Your father is your shelter.

- Anna Carr

❧

He spreadeth fast food before us; he buyeth us souvenirs. His good humor and patience rarely end. Surely all of our memories will be happy ones, and we will love God forever and ever.

- Eva Allen

❧

A dad's love waits up when the rest of the world has already turned out the lights.

- Diana Manning

Every dad, if he takes time out of his busy life to reflect upon his fatherhood, can learn ways to become an even better dad.

- Jack Baker

A man's desire for a son is usually nothing but the wish to duplicate himself in order that such a remarkable pattern may not be lost to the world.

- Helen Rowland

Every one expects to go further than his father went; every one expects to be better than he was born and every generation has one big impulse in its heart—to exceed all the other generations of the past in all the things that make life worth living.

- William Allen White

It is a great moment in life when a father sees a son grow taller than he or reach farther than he.

- Richard L. Evans

My father was an amazing man. The older I got, the smarter he got.

- Mark Twain

There's so much negative imagery of black fatherhood. I've got tons of friends that are doing the right thing by their kids, and doing the right thing as a father—and how come that's not as newsworthy?

- Will Smith

&

The greatest thing about tomorrow is, I will be better than I am today. And that's how I look at my life. I will be a better golfer, I will be a better person, I will be a better father, I will be a better husband, I will be a better friend. That's the beauty of tomorrow.

- Tiger Woods

Meet the Greatest Father in the World

Get to Know Jesus Christ

God is the greatest Father in the world. He gave His Son, Jesus Christ, so that we all could have eternal life and have the assurance of going to Heaven. If you are reading this book and do not know the Lord Jesus Christ as your personal Saviour, please read the following:

1. **Accept the fact that you are a sinner, and that you have broken God's law.** The Bible says in Ecclesiastes 7:20: *"For there is not a just man upon earth that doeth good, and sinneth not."* Romans 3:23: *"For all have sinned and come short of the glory of God."*

2. **Accept the fact that there is a penalty for sin.** The Bible states in Romans 6:23: *"For the wages of sin is death..."*

3. **Accept the fact that you are on the road to hell.**

Jesus Christ said in Matthew 10:28: *"And fear not them which kill the body, but are not able to kill the soul: but rather fear him which is able to destroy both soul and body in hell."*

The Bible says in Revelation 21:8: *"But the fearful, and unbelieving, and the abominable, and murderers, and whoremongers and sorcerers, and idolaters, and all liars, shall have their part in the lake which burneth with fire and brimstone: which is the second death."*

4. **Accept the fact that you cannot do anything to save yourself!** The Bible states in Ephesians 2:8, 9: *"For by grace are ye saved through faith: and that not of yourselves: it is a gift of God. Not of works, lest any man should boast."*

5. **Accept the fact that God loves you more than you love yourself, and that He wants to save you from hell.** *"For God so loved the world, that He gave His only begotten Son, that whosoever believeth in Him should not perish, but have everlasting life"* (John 3:16).

6. With these facts in mind, please repent of your sins, believe on the Lord Jesus Christ and pray and ask Him to come into your heart and save you this very moment.

The Bible states in the book of Romans 10:9, 13: *"That if thou shalt confess with thy mouth the Lord Jesus, and shalt believe in thine heart that God hath raised Him from the dead, thou shalt be saved." "For whosoever shall call upon the name of the Lord shall be saved."*

7. If you are willing to trust Christ as your Saviour please pray with me the following prayer:

Heavenly Father, I realize that I am a sinner and that I have sinned against you. For Jesus Christ's sake, please forgive me of all of my sins. I now believe with all of my heart that Jesus Christ died, was buried, and rose again for me. Lord Jesus, please come into my heart, save my soul, change my life, and fill me with your Holy Ghost today and forever. Amen.

Great Resources to Help You Become a Great Father

BOOKS

1. *Successfully Raising Young Black Men*, by Kevin D. Barnes, Sr.

2. *Fatherhood By George: Hard-Won Advice on Being a Dad*, by George Foreman

3. *Better Dads, Stronger Sons: How Fathers Can Guide Boys to Become Men of Character*, by Rick Johnson

4. *Bringing Up Boys*, by James C. Dobson

5. *The New Strong-Willed Child*, by James C. Dobson

6. *Parents' Answer Book*, by James C. Dobson

7. *The Fatherhood Principle*, by Myles Munroe

8. *Fathering Like the Father: Becoming the Dad God*

Wants You to Be, by Kenneth Gangel and Jeffrey Gangel

9. *Fatherhood*, by Bill Cosby

10. *Step Up to the Plate, Dad!*, by R.V. Brown

11. *Wild Things: The Art of Nurturing Boys*, by Stephen James and David Thomas

12. *The Power Of Dad: The Influence Of Today's Fathers and The Destiny Of Their Children*, by Brian Pruitt

13. *Being a Good Dad: When You Didn't Have One*, by Tim Wesemann

14. *Wisdom of Our Fathers: Lessons and Letters from Daughters and Sons*, by Tim Russert

15. *Father Force*, by Phillip Davis

16. *They Call Me Dad: The Practical Art of Effective Fathering*, by Ken Canfield

17. *Head of the Family: Christian Fatherhood in the Modern World*, by Clayton C. Barbeau

18. *Becoming Dad: Black Men and the Journey to Fatherhood*, by Leonard Pitts Jr.

19. *Be a Father to Your Child: Real Talk from Black Men on Family, Love, and Fatherhood*, by April R. Silver

20. *Fathered by God : Learning What Your Dad Could Never Teach You*, by John Eldredge

Great Resources to Help You Become a Great Father

WEBSITES

1. www.Fathers.com
2. www.DearPapa.org
3. www.SuccessfullyRaisingYoungBlackMen.com
4. www.Fatherville.com
5. www.BlackFatherhoodToday.com
6. www.FatherhoodInstitute.org
7. www.BlackFathersHallofFame.com
8. www.FathersNetwork.org
9. www.ChristianFathers.com
10. www.FathersWorld.com
11. www.AfricanFathers.org
12. www.FatherMag.com

Great Resources to Help You Become a Great Father

MINISTRIES/ ORGANIZATIONS

1. Fathers.com/National Center for Fathering
   P.O. Box 413888
   Kansas City, MO 64141
   1-800-593-DADS
   dads@fathers.com
   www.fathers.com

2. National Fatherhood Initiative
   101 Lake Forest Boulevard
   Suite 360
   Gaithersburg, Maryland 20877
   p: 301.948.0599
   f: 301.948.4325
   www.fatherhood.org

3. InsideOut Dad
   A Reentry Program for Incarcerated Fathers
   kgosnell@fatherhood.org
   p: 240.912.1283
   f: 301.948.4325
   www.fatherhood.org/InsideOutDad/

4. American Coalition for Fathers and Children
   1718 M. St. NW #187
   Washington, DC 20036
   p: 800.978.3237
   f: 703.433.9023
   info@acfc.org
   www.acfc.org

5. Center on Fathers, Families, and Public Policy
   23 N. Pinckney Street
   Suite 210
   Madison, WI 53703
   p: 608.257.3148
   f: 608.257.4686
   boggess@cffpp.org
   www.cffpp.org

6. The Father Project
   mark@fatherproject.com
   www.fatherproject.com

7. Black Fatherhood Foundation
   www.blackfatherhoodfoundation.org
   info@blackfatherhoodfoundation.org

FOR MORE INFORMATION OR TO HEAR REV. DANIEL WHITE, JR., SINGING SONGS FROM HIS GOSPEL ALBUM TITLED *GET READY,* VISIT: www.GodHasSmiledonMe.com

6192699R0

Made in the USA
Lexington, KY
28 July 2010